Jane & Frank,
God bless you both!
enjoy the ride... Love,
Nancy
11·13·15

Hit Back, Hit Hard, and Dream On

Nancy Karlson Bridge

Published by Nancy Karlson Bridge.

Created with Verbii.com (Design, Formatting, Ebook Conversion and Printing)

Author photo, back cover collage and hand puppet photo courtesy of Ashly Alexander. Big fat crayon photo courtesy of Glenwood Jackson. Snake photos courtesy of Alan Leo.
Head shot page 110, courtesy of Robert Grasmere.

ISBN: 978-0-9903901-0-7 (hard cover)
ISBN: 978-0-9903901-1-4 (softcover)
ISBN: 978-0-9903901-3-8 (epub iTunes)
ISBN: 978-0-9903901-4-5 (mobi Kindle)
ISBN: 978-0-9903901-2-1 (softcover spanish)
ISBN: 978-0-9903901-5-2 (Audio/Read by the Author English)
ISBN: 978-0-9903901-6-9 (Audio/Read by the Author Spanish)

First Edition

Library of Congress Control Number: 2014915797

Copies are available at special rates for bulk orders.

Contact the sales team at sales@hitbackhithard.com

The Players I'd Like to Thank

Mona Lindblom, Dan Bridge, Christina Gosnell, Natallia Ivchankova, Stacey Murrow, Patrick Brennan, Werner Erhard, Natasha Sandy, Layne and Michael Humphrey, Pastor Tony Smith, Tracy Honafius, Linda Slawski, Hugh Hefner, Julia Roberts, Liv Tyler, Christine Kloser, Marlene Oulton, Mark Matousek, Cindy Rogers, Dianne Yospe, Robert (Kelly) Kelleher, Laura Helen Kaufman, Horst Rechelbacher, David Wagner, Richard Millstein, Jerry Bridge, Susan and Steve Haveard, Jazmine Thomas, Sharon So, Jeanne O'Conor, Syd Wright, Ashly Alexander, Mike Linnan, Ron and Sally Lesser, Reba Forney, Andrea Balt and Joey Kramer.

Thank you for loving me, supporting me, enlightening me, saving my badass, teaching me, believing in me and showing me all that I can be. I love you all dearly and remain yours in service for a brighter and bolder planet that believes in love.

The Supporting Cast:

You! Thank you for buying and reading this book and believing in the beauty of your own dreams. They've been divinely placed within your heart and you are well equipped to manifest each and every one of them. Dare to believe and wonder and fall down. What matters is that you get back up.

Your stage is set. The cast and crew are ready. Write it, wish it, believe it and dream on, dream until your dreams come true, they may be closer than you think.

Foreword

As the title suggests, this book is about fighting the good fight and finding yourself in the process. It is about having the courage to speak up against injustices, of any kind, and taking up noble causes like loving people for a lifetime.

It's about brave choices and uncertain outcomes. It's about fierce hearts and those who dare to dream. It's about epiphanies and enlightment, living powerfully and passionately. It's about choosing your own path, especially when doubted.

It's about living your own life on purpose, and breaking the chains that bind. It's about beautifully and magnificently sharing your self, as if it mattered. It is about carrying a torch, letting it burn brightly and passing it on.

It's about heartache and victory and God thoughts.

It's about not selling out, especially on your self. It's about setting the record straight, letting the truth set you free, and hopefully, set a few others free along the way.

These are the stories, as I remember them, about my time with Aerosmith, being a Playboy Bunny, a reluctant student, and a beautiful young girl with epilepsy.

There are more than a few people in this book, spanning five decades, who have graced the covers of magazines; however, those nearest and dearest to me can be found in my own backyard.

Chapter Set List

Bonus Tracks:

www.hitbackhithard.com
www.epilepsy.com
www.abilitiesnetwork.org
www.wernererhard.com
www.landmarkworldwide.com
www.pastortonysmith.com
www.rachelsvineyard.com
www.andreabalt.com
www.MarleneOulton.com
www.glenwoodjacksonphotography.com

Curb Notes from Nancy's 7,000 mile road trip available at
www.hitbackhithard.com.

Introduction and Dedication

In the summer of 2009, I was reunited with someone I barely knew back in the 1970's, Laura Helen Kaufman. Laura worked for Steve Leber and David Krebs, two of the most powerful and influential rock band managers who ever lived. She was the top publicist in the Leber-Krebs Management firm and worth her weight in gold. All the tasks, agendas, careers and lives that Laura impacted would make your head spin. Her work directly influenced the careers of Aerosmith, Ted Nugent, The New York Dolls and Lynyrd Skynyrd. Other rock acts she coddled and nurtured along the way included Judas Priest, Peter Frampton, Styx, Motorhead and Iron Maiden. She managed them all with grace, dignity and fierce determination.

To see her in action, twenty-four hours a day, seven days a week was a miracle to behold. She didn't know the meaning of the word 'no.' Anything was possible and nothing out of reach. Some even thought her to have a direct line to Divinity. Maybe she did.

Laura managed nearly all aspects of each and every person's career she worked with. Tour details, press releases, press coverage, personal crises, hotel accommodations for large groups of ungrateful people never failing to notice what wasn't right in their hotel room or backstage. Broken hearts, broken dreams, and even broken down doors, were her specialty. Plane delays, rerouting dozens of people and their baggage and equipment on the spot of a dime, no one did it better than her. She was the task master for several musical acts, simultaneously.

Laura Kaufman managed all these groups of people and their entourages, without the use of Facebook, Twitter or text messaging. There were no cell phones or personal computers. With the proficiency of a Steve Jobs running Apple, Laura skillfully and giftedly accomplished all of these feats without the help of any of our current electronic devices. Her voice was loud enough. She was well respected in the music industry. Legendary.

I didn't know Laura well at the time, back in the 1970's, but she was a household name in my circle of friends. Her name was dropped in almost every conversation I ever heard concerning Aerosmith, and the business of the band. It was believed that Laura Kaufman could and would do just about anything to ensure their success. Laura was the instrumental force behind the band and all of its publicity. She was the one opening each and every door for the band's climb to success. She took life and her job on like the unstoppable locomotive of a train. And Laura made sure that train kept a rollin'.

Laura, a pint sized native New Yorker who could take on any football linebacker with grace and ease, was already well known in the music industry as one tough cookie, someone you couldn't say no to. She almost always got what she wanted. Her passion for music found her at a young post pubescent age, in her own Greenwich Village neighborhood. She loved the scene, the rock scene and the music that fueled it.

From late 1974 to 1977, I was the girlfriend of Joey Kramer, the drummer of Aerosmith. During this time my circle of friends and family were the band and a few people I worked with at Playboy of Boston.

Bob Kelleher, affectionately called Kelly, found me on Facebook in July, 2009. Kelly was the Road Manager and Tour Director for Aerosmith in the 1970's. He too, was the best in the business. I knew Kelly well and loved him dearly.

Kelly had a big heart and more than his share of managing details while we, or the band – without wives and girlfriends – were out on the road touring. Kelly was an attractive, dark haired man with a big Bostonian brawl and a size to match. He was rarely found without something kind to say, or pen and paper in hand to take down a note. His mere chest size alone was like the fifty yard line on a football field with players ready to roar.

Kelly was responsible for just about everything with the tours, once we were out of town. With great talent and finesse, Kelly attended to Steven Tyler, Joe Perry, Brad Whitford, Tom Hamilton, and Joey Kramer. He oversaw the road crew, travel arrangements for the band and crew, promoters, hotels, wives and girlfriends being happy, groupies, drug dealers, celebrity access and backstage guests at all the shows, expenses, per diems, cars, trucks and airplanes. He took care of all of it, and us, like a rockstar.

Even after Joey and I broke up, Kelly took the time to send me a birthday card that year. "Happy Birthday," it read, "This bud's for you!" It had a red rose bud on the front. That was Kelly, always ready with a kind word and a shout of optimism.

I was thrilled to hear from him in the summer of 2009. It was great catching up with him after all these years. He suggested that Laura Kaufman and I become friends on Facebook. I couldn't imagine why Kelly would suggest that Laura and I become 'friends' on Facebook. She and I weren't close back in the day. I only knew of her, but hardly knew her.

My boyfriend, Joey Kramer, knew her well and spoke with her often, mostly on the telephone from our apartment in Brookline, Massachusetts, back in the 1970's. The long distance calls with Joey, from New York, where Laura lived and worked, were always lengthy. I would make sure everything was quiet in our home during those calls so that Joey could express himself powerfully to her with regard to his career. I wanted him to know he had my love and support too.

Laura was Joey's sounding board, a pledged-to-his success advocate, and it didn't hurt that she understood his Yiddish. I was a novice. I liked her because she liked him and he always seemed to feel better after talking with her.

Joey felt hidden and unheard behind his drums. He wanted to be out in front more and gain as much attention as the rest of the band, especially Steven and Joe. It was an impossible dream, but he always went for it. Joey was much closer to Tom and Brad, bassist and rhythm guitarist, than he was to the front men, Steven Tyler and Joe Perry.

Joey was a squeaky wheel whenever he talked to Laura. It was understood, in Steven's words, that the band was like a car and Joey was the engine. It was his job to drive the band.

Joey believed that he was important too and people should know it; that there should be articles written about him and his contributions to driving the band. He felt it was Laura's job to make that happen, as she did so many other things. It was agreed that she alone was responsible for all the hype about the band. If anyone could shed light on Joey it would be Laura; she took everything on as if she were driving a fast sports car to heaven.

Laura arranged an interview for Joey with Circus Magazine in March of 1976. The article wasn't printed until November, 1976, eight months after it was recorded on the phone. The interview took place in the kitchen of our home on James Street, in Brookline, MA. I gave Joey tremendous privacy during that call because he was so damn nervous and excited to be interviewed. He was one confident man, and when he got off the phone, I knew from his face and demeanor that it went well.

The article was titled, "Different Drummer/ Why Aerosmith's Joey Kramer is Media Shy." Of the five pictures included in the article, only one was of Joey. The other pictures were, of course, of Steven Tyler and Joe Perry.

Several of the printed statements made by Joey in the article authentically depicted what he believed about life, love, fortune and fame. He often said these things to me.

"Once you start to believe that, (you're something bigger than life) once you start to tell a lie long enough, you start to believe it – and that's how these guys start projecting images. The people I admire are the ones who are the biggest stars, but who keep themselves together."

The article also quoted information from Joey's official bio, written by the Leber-Krebs Company, and shared his personal motto: "Don't give up until you get what you want – keep punching."

How often I had heard this one and the one that followed, "If you want something bad enough you can get it, but you have to want it that bad."

Another favorite teaching Joey did his best to inculcate in me was also in the article, "Whatever you put into something, that's what you get out of it."

Towards the end of the interview Joey admits for all to read "that, he is, for the first time in his life, in love – from the tips of my toes to the tips of my hair." The article goes on to say that "Much of his happiness is the result of a woman [Nancy Carlson]." That would be me, last name spelled incorrectly.

"She made me realize a lot of heavy things about myself. Falling in love also gave me confidence. I've been living with my old lady for two years now, and neither one of us has the desire to get married. But as long as we both feel this way we'll stay together. Besides the band, it's the only thing that has meaning for me. We spend so much time on the road, and there are few people you can relate to and get to know as a person. I think that's why a lot of us get married so young in my business. Because it's not an easy thing to have security, and you think about losing it and try to secure it the best you can."

However, eight months is a lifetime in the world of rock and roll. Things had changed drastically between Joey and I. Tom and Terry had married, as did Brad and Lori and Joe and Elyssa. Steven and Joey were the last two unmarried members of the band. And Joey was pushing me for marriage.

I was hurt and reluctant to give an answer to a question that had not yet been asked in an official and engaging way; I wanted him to drop a knee and sweetly ask me, not just talk about it.

The article in the November 1976 issue of Circus Magazine was old news now, but it said to the world that we didn't want to be married.

Still reeling from my unexpressed emotions about the article and how much things had changed for Joey and me since the recording of that interview, Joey made an unexpected announcement to the press on November 13, 1976. We were backstage, just before a concert at the Boston Garden, when Joey decided to take his shot at big news coverage. He told reporters that we were engaged to be married. I could not believe those words came out of his mouth.

Joey had not yet popped the question to me, in that happy ending story book way of his. I don't remember if it was The Boston Globe or The Herald that he told, but it was uncomfortable for everyone. It was the first night of three sold out concerts at the Garden. Joe Perry, there with his mom and sister, had just been asked about the death of his father.

Joey spoke without thinking.

It wasn't that we hadn't been talking about marriage, having purchased property in New Hampshire and planning to build our new home there, we just hadn't sweetly sealed the deal yet. I was expecting romance and a big beautiful Joey moment when the time came.

How could he make such a brash and unplanned remark about the state of our relationship like he was talking about a new sports car he had just purchased? I was flabbergasted. He had not yet proposed to me and there was no ring.

I could not bring myself to confirm or deny an engagement of marriage to Joey, not that anyone was asking. My feelings weren't important to the reporter or to Joey – so it seemed, in that moment. It was not a romantic, however botched, proposal of marriage Joey made to me. It was a look at me – I can do it too – spotlight seeking disaster.

And the look on Joey's face afterwards, was like "Holy shit man, what have I done now?"

Good show, very bad night for me.

Thirty eight years later, in 2009, I received a Facebook friend request from Laura Helen Kaufman, at Kelly's suggestion. I wondered what we could possibly have to talk about after all these years. I knew she thought well of me and believed that what Joey and I shared would withstand the test of time. It almost did.

At that time, I was in the middle of moving into my newly purchased home in July of 2009, and working fulltime. While enthusiastically unpacking boxes in my bedroom, I ran with exuberance and abandon, toes first, into a heavy box on the floor marked as "books." I broke two toes on my right foot. Unable to stand at work, which my job required, I began to spend time on the internet with my toes iced and elevated. It was there that I discovered Joey Kramer, my old flame, had written a book.

On crutches and driving with two broken pedal toes, I made my way to the local bookstore to purchase Joey's book.

I was so damn proud of him. Good for him, he's finally on the front cover and it's his story. I could hardly wait to get back to my car and begin thumbing through the pages, right there in the Borders' parking lot.

Oh, the feel of a hardback book, and this one written by someone I knew intimately and loved dearly. What a success you now are, Joey Kramer! Yes, good for you!

Still sitting in my car, I looked at the chapter titles, number of pages and the many pages of pictures. Then it occurred to me that I might be in the book, maybe a small mention, after all, we'd spent relevant, important and treasured time together in the 1970's. We'd shared three homes together in Boston and had planned to build our little dream castle in the woods of New Hampshire.

Our relationship had occurred during the time the band saw the most growth with popularity and sky rocketing sales. Joey and I, as individuals, also grew enormously during that time. We'd been in touch and seen each other over the years that followed, always a warm and special occasion. Maybe, just maybe, he had something very kind to say about me, however brief it may be.

As I was flipping through the pages toward the end of book, still parked in my car, the words "my girlfriend, Cindy, had her epileptic seizure" jumped out at me. Oh no, I thought. Who is he talking about?

Frantically, I thumbed through the pages quickly now, searching for a context and what girlfriend with epilepsy was he was making reference to. No, it couldn't be me, but how many people with epilepsy can one person date?

Next I saw, "My girlfriend Cindy Oster, the Playboy Bunny, was there, too." No. What are the odds of Joey Kramer dating more than one Playboy Bunny with epilepsy?

Holy crap. What had he done?

The next paragraph describes an event in our Brookline apartment at 19 James Street, as he says it happened, while he was away, on tour. "And Cindy was sort of supervising and painting some of the walls. Cindy was epileptic and had to take medication to control it."

"She and Scott were, of course, also consuming quite a bit of blow, and Cindy had forgotten to take her pills. Scott described to me how he heard this crash, ran into the next room, and there was gorgeous Cindy, lying on the floor and frothing at the mouth, her eyes rolled back in her head. Scott immediately called 911, but when the medics and cops arrived, he remembered the huge pile of blow sitting on the coffee table, lines all laid out. So he left Cindy shaking on the floor and the cops banging on the door while he ran around the apartment and hid all the coke."

My jaw hit the floorboard of the car and I no longer held any interest in reading his book. I was shocked, perturbed and deeply insulted, not just for myself, but for all the people who suffer with disabilities. How dare he refer to people with epilepsy as epileptics, like referring to people who have cancer as cancerites? How dare he talk about frothing at the mouth during a seizure, which he never witnessed?

What had he done?

Less than two hundred years ago, people afflicted with epilepsy were burned at the stake in New England because the society at the time thought that they were demonically possessed. What possessed Joey, to portray me and our relationship, in such a demeaning and unflattering light as this?

Who could possibly understand the full range of emotions I was suddenly flooded with? Laura Helen Kaufman, someone who was there at the time! I accepted her friend request and she was just what the doctor ordered; sane, rational consoling for my heart and mind.

I last saw Joey backstage at a concert at the Nissan Pavilion in Virginia, 1997. We talked in a small private room for so long that the band delayed the plane waiting to take them back to Boston. He told me about his nervous breakdown in Miami and how his band mates rallied around him refusing to let him be replaced by another drummer – in the studio or otherwise. Finally, he had gotten the love, peace and respect he had so desperately yearned for his entire life. I was happy for him and more than willing to listen to and share the celebration of his personal and professional breakthrough.

What I'm about to tell you is still incredibly difficult for me to talk about.

After accepting Laura Kaufman's friend request in 2009, we began writing email letters to each other, almost weekly, until the time of her death, March 3, 2012. She became my cherished friend, mentor and writing inspiration. It was through our treasured friendship and the intimate writing of long letters that I was able to forgive Joey for what he'd written about me in his book.

In 2012, I was in the early stages of writing this book and at that time, I was writing from an unhealed, reactive stance in response to the untrue and ludicrous things Joey Kramer wrote about "Cindy Oster" in his book, "Hit Hard" – a story of hitting rock bottom at the top.

Laura Kaufman knew the truth about both my relationship with Joey and how selfishly rock stars can sometimes behave. Laura incessantly encouraged me to keep writing.

Laura, also a writer, had completed two novels at the time of her death, "Rock in a Hard Place," named after her endless devotion and love of Aerosmith and "Birds of a Feather" about what she knew best, rock and roll. She was a fantastic story teller.

Unfortunately, to the best of my knowledge neither book has yet to be published. I tell you this because having read the manuscript for "Rock in a Hard Place," I would love to see her surviving sister be able to publish her rock hard and dedicated work.

In Laura's last letter to me, just a few days before her passing, she closed her loving message with these words, "Just remember, Nan, writers write, no matter what. Love, Laura."

The completion of this book, "Hit Back, Hit Hard, and Dream On" is the "no matter what" part.

Laura – This is for you...I love you with all my heart. Thanks for helping me find the strength, courage and love to finish this story and lifelong dream of becoming a published author.

Rocking and writing on, every damn day.

I love you from here to eternity and beyond,

Nan

Track **1**

DREAM ON - How the Hell Did We Get Here?

Baltimore, Maryland – late November, 1975

"**D**on't bands ever get bored playing the same songs night after night?" Mom asked Joey. We were still sitting at the Thanksgiving Day table at Mom's house in Baltimore after a fine meal. Mom, in her strictly Southern tradition, had the table set with all the trimmings and frills befitting of true southern hospitality. We had traveled from Boston to Baltimore to be with Mom for the holiday and she was meeting my boyfriend, Joey Kramer, for the first time.

Mom was very interested in getting to know the person that I had been living with for almost a year in Boston. I felt proud and dearly loved the fact that Mom was taking such a genuine interest in Joey and his career. No one in my hometown of Baltimore knew much about the band called Aerosmith, and it usually took a great deal of effort to explain the spelling of the band's name and that they were a musical group from Boston.

What kind of group?

What do they play?

Are they hard rock?

These were the usual questions I'd encounter whenever I tried to tell people who my boyfriend was and what he did for a living. I have to admit that I was always a bit embarrassed trying to explain it. Joey wasn't famous: he just played drums in this band.

1

I had been a student in Baltimore and had transferred to a small college in Boston. I was a Playboy Bunny at Playboy of Boston. People could understand those facts; most people recognized anything having to do with Playboy.

Joey answered Mom telling her, "I don't get bored even though we play the same songs night after night. It's different every night because the audience is always different."

Mom thought about this for a few minutes while fiddling with her fork. Then she asked him, "Where are you heading; what are the plans for the future of the band?"

I felt nervous, as if my Pop were sitting there in the room with us about to ask Joey what his intentions were for his daughter.

"Where are we headed?" Joey repeated. "Well, nothing's really moving right now. We just released a single, called 'You See Me Crying' and not much is happening with it. It hasn't made the charts. We need a hit single or something, to get things going."

We left the dinner table and moved into the living room. I could tell that Mom was still thinking. Mom was always advancing things to the next level, it was in her nature.

"What about that song, 'Dream On', it's such a good song." I could hear in her voice the genuine affinity she was cultivating for Joey and his music.

"We released that two years ago and it did alright", Joey answered. "But not much is happening at the moment. "

There was a longer pause and I could almost see the wheels in Mom's head spinning. I didn't know what she would say next, but I knew it would be a thoughtful response, offered with great care and concern. Mom was a manager for C&P Telephone Company in Baltimore and it was her job to trouble-shoot and problem-solve and she did it quite well. It didn't matter to her that she was one of the first women to hold her position in the company; her attitude was that this change for women was long overdue, and she could do most things far better than most of the men who had previously held these high level positions in the telephone company.

2

"Do bands ever re-release a single? Could you bring that song out again and try to push the band's recognition?" Whoa. I didn't expect that question. Neither did Joey from the look on his face. Why hadn't someone thought of that before? It hadn't occurred to anyone before because it was a ground breaking idea, the kind that came so easily for Mom.

Joey started to twitch as he often did when he got excited or nervous. His right eyebrow would rise up and down and his nostrils would flare and join the dance as he sniffled and cleared his throat. His right shoulder would bob up and down trying to reach his right ear. It would last for minutes and he would keep speaking, voice a little higher and always on time to a beat that no one could hear, but you could feel. It was an endearing habit and I loved that about him. He was my drummer boy and I loved him with all my heart. I could tell he was working his way right into Mom's heart too.

"Wow. That's a great idea. I'll uh, I'll uh, have to call my managers when we get back to see if we can do that." I could tell that Joey was really impressed with Mom and perhaps even loved her daughter a little more, seeing the genetic line.

We got back to our apartment at 19 James Street in Brookline Friday night. First thing Saturday morning Joey called Davis Krebs, manager for the band in New York, to tell him about the idea of re-releasing 'Dream On' as a single record.

He was calling David from the wall phone in our kitchen, and I was standing nearby in the breakfast nook. I was being very quiet and smiling from ear to ear. I was so proud of him. I knew this idea was almost like launching a man to the moon, and it took great effort to contain my excitement for him. Joey, drummer for the band, always in the back shadows, not a singer or a song writer, was changing the course of history for five guys from Boston.

Joey got off the phone and shouted, "David thinks it's a great idea!"

Oh my Lord, David thinks it's a great idea. We were jumping up and down, shaking the kitchen floor. It was like being at the Indianapolis 500 auto race and Joey's car was in the lead. A dream was about to come true. Joey and his band would make it!

3

Davis Krebs convinced Columbia Records to re-release 'Dream On' as a single record in December. We watched the song climb the music charts with a bullet and by early 1976 it was on its way to making the top ten list of Billboard. Even though the song had been originally released two years earlier, with this second release the band was catapulted to unprecedented success.

In Boston, in January of 1976, we were living a fairly normal life in our beautiful first floor apartment in Brookline, just around the corner from Coolidge Corner, except that, Joey now had more money than he knew what to do with. He had received his first huge royalty check, more than $200,000, for album sales from the previous year. We had more cars than places to park them. Joey had to rent spaces in a nearby garage for two of the cars because our rented apartment only came with one covered parking space, behind our building. Street parking was usually unavailable, not that Joey would have parked any of his cars on the street.

1975 and 1976 had been horrendous years of working and touring, only to have fortune and fame come knocking at our doorstep, suddenly and without warning. The band was used to fighting hard and struggling endlessly to be heard. Now, Aerosmith was getting airplay, everywhere. Talk was that the next album might be shipped 'Gold' and that the last album, 'Toys in the Attic', might go Platinum with 1,000,000 copies being sold.

By January of 1977, we had all paid our dues, band members and their significant others, many times over, for the life and things we were now supposed to be enjoying. I had been to see a doctor in Brookline, who said I was suffering from extreme stress and nervousness, and he prescribed little yellow pills, 5mg valium for me and lots of rest. The valium, he said, would also serve as an additional anticonvulsant along with the medication I already took for epilepsy.

I took a temporary leave of absence from the Playboy Club to reflect, recover, and try to regain balance from this wild merry-go-round ride we had been on. Joey went into pre-production. I sat down to ponder; how the hell did we get here?

Track **2**

OH SUSIE Q - Meeting the Band

I graduated from high school in 1973 by the skin of my teeth. Uncontrollable epileptic seizures, deep emotional wounds, and feeling stigmatized by epilepsy and by divorcing parents kept me from attending classes for most of my senior year. I officially dropped out in October and returned in April to work my tail off to graduate with my graduating class. When I crossed the stage to receive my diploma I was very proud of my achievement and pregnant. Roe v Wade had just been decided and I chose to terminate the pregnancy.

On July 1, 1973, I was hired to work as a waitress in a members only men's key club called "The Gas Lamp." It was similar to the Playboy Club but much more conservative in costume, attire and atmosphere. The 1940's style exclusive men's club was owned and operated by one of Baltimore's historic five star restaurants, The Eager House. It was there that I first laid eyes on Susan.

Paul Souza, general manager for both businesses, was waiting to introduce us. We were standing in the restaurant's kitchen service area where the servers and upstairs waitresses from the Gas Lamp picked up the food to be served. Susan had her back to us. Paul was telling me that Susie (I've always preferred to call her Susan) would train me and show me the ropes.

Although Susan had her back to us, she had the full attention of everyone working in the kitchen. She was wearing an emerald green velvet abbreviated Playboy Bunny like costume with a flattering stiff black chiffon bow where the Playboy Bunny white cotton tail would be. The costume rode up high on her perfect derriere, clung tightly at the waist, and was held in place with a twenty inch zipper. She was also wearing matching emerald green high heeled spiked shoes and jet black hose. Her long blond hair grazed the top of the back of her costume. She was gorgeous and I was just looking at the back of her.

Paul Souza went on to say that I was to shadow her for the next two nights. He told me to just wear hot pants (very short shorts), a well fitted blouse, black hose and heels until my abbreviated costume was ready.

Still with her back to me, Susan slowly turned around to see who the new kid was she'd be working with and I think my jaw must have dropped. My Lord, she was even prettier from the front. She had a beautiful white infectious smile, deep dark brown eyes and flawless skin. Like the cooks in the kitchen, I couldn't help but be mesmerized by her full breasts resting comfortably on the top of her costume. She was the most beautiful woman I'd ever seen. Realizing that I too was looking a little too long at her chest, Susan laughed and said, "It's okay, I get that a lot. They're real."

She told me to meet her at 5:00 pm the next day, look hot and be ready to learn, quickly. She said I was a little young and she had no time for hand holding; I'd better pick things up right away. Susan was kind and straight forward.

I was a quick study and Susan was pleased. I trained well, including learning how to make a Caesar salad from scratch, tableside, my first night. Her tips were doubled both nights.

Susan was five years older than me and well experienced. At 22, she had already worked as a Playboy Bunny in Baltimore, Miami and Jamaica. Her belt was well notched with actors, musicians and entertainers who had fallen prey to her charms.

Susan invited me to join her for the Fourth of July weekend in Ocean City, Maryland. We'd take her car and leave after work. I was so impressed by her that I would have followed her anywhere. She was like the big sister I never had.

We began the three hour drive to Ocean City at about 11:00 pm in Susan's white Cadillac that had a black vinyl top and vanity license plates that read "SUSIE Q." Susan was a bit tired from work and said we should listen to some peppy music to help keep us awake for the ride. She put in a cassette tape of Aerosmith's album and handed the cassette cover over to me. She asked if I was familiar with their music and I shook my head.

Susan asked if I'd heard their song "Dream On" on the radio and I told her I had, once. I checked with her to see if I could ask her a few questions about dating and sex and she said yes, but I'd have to wait. She had to hear at least this one song, "Make It." She pumped up the volume and began to rock to and fro in her seat while still driving the car. She instructed me to look at the band's pictures in the cassette case that I was still holding and asked if I agreed with her that they were cute. I didn't particularly think so but I said yes, hoping we could get to my questions.

She pointed to Steven Tyler, front man and lead singer for the band and said, "He's mine. That's who I'm going to see in Ocean City." I asked her how long she'd known him and she said they hadn't met yet. She said, "Trust me. I'll meet him tomorrow night at the show." I didn't doubt her.

Finally, about an hour outside of Ocean City, we got to my questions. They were all about the how's and why's of sex. Susan patiently answered each and every one of my curiosities leaving me clueless no more.

We spent the next day, Saturday, at the beach playing in waves and floating on rafts in the ocean. Susan didn't like my two piece bathing suit and gave me one of her bikinis to wear, assuring me that when it got wet, her white crocheted bikini would shrink to fit my less than hers, voluptuous shape.

In the late afternoon we primped and purred and took our time getting ready for the concert. We drove to the Ocean City Convention Center, where the band Aerosmith was playing, and Susan parked the car under a tall street lamp in the Convention Center's parking lot. We entered the arena while the band was already playing and within minutes Susan had us standing right in front of the stage.

The attraction between Susan and the band's lead singer, Steven Tyler, was immediate and intense. He sang directly to her bending the microphone stand that was draped with long scarves down to her chest, which was resting comfortably on the front edge of the stage. She lifted her body to meet his every breath. Her performance was as professional and coy as his. I felt like a voyeur watching two people make love in public.

About an hour later I was bored silly and had to pee. I told Susan I'd be right back. When I returned about fifteen minutes later, the show was over, the band had left the stage and Susan was gone. The crowd was leaving and roadies were packing up the band's equipment. Susan was nowhere to be found. I searched the bathrooms, the parking lot and no Susan. I had to find her; I didn't have a car or the address of where we were staying and I was underage.

Her car was still parked under the street lamp on the parking lot. Then it occurred to me that she must be with Steven, still inside the building. The only place I hadn't looked was backstage. Great, how do I get backstage at a rock concert? This was no time to be timid or polite; I had to get back into that building and find Susan. I made my way back into the arena and walked through the Back Stage Access Only area as if I owned the place. I opened the first door I came to and thank God there was Susan sitting on Steven's lap slowly and deeply kissing him.

"Hi," I said. "Boy, am I glad to see you!"

Susan said, "Hi yourself. We're going back to their hotel with them."

"Okay, for what?" I asked.

"We're gonna have a little party and just hang out."

What choice did I have? We rode with them in regular cars, not limos, to the Ramada Inn in Fenwick, leaving Susan's car on the Convention Center's parking lot. Susan rode with Steven and I rode with Tom, Brad and Joey. When we got to the hotel Susan said she was going to Steven's room and would I mind staying the night in Brad and Joey's room. Again, what choice did I have? I was underage, without a car, no credit card and knew no one else in Ocean City besides Susan.

Brad and Joey were sharing a room with two double beds. I wanted to sleep on the floor between the two beds but Brad insisted that I take half of his bed. I eluded his advances by talking rapidly about everything under the sun I could think of until he fell asleep. Then, I quietly made my way with pillow in hand to the floor.

The next morning we all met in the hotel lobby. The boys were leaving for their next show in another town and Steven arranged to have someone drive us back to Susan's car.

This began the first of many wild times with Susan. She and Steven started "dating" a few months after the Fourth of July weekend in Ocean City and I'd tag along with her to the shows to see him. Often times there would be a third rider in the car with us: a freshly baked oven roasted turkey that Susan had made, just for Steven. It was his favorite.

After about a year of attending shows with her when they played anywhere near Baltimore, Susan and Steven began telling me that Joey, the drummer in the band, thought that I was really cute and would like to go out with me. I wasn't interested. They begged me to just have a drink with him. Reluctantly, I finally agreed.

The band was playing at the Convention Center in downtown Baltimore. I agreed to have a drink with him at their hotel after the show. I was not excited about it, but I had given my word to have just that one drink.

During the show, Susan and I were onstage, to the left of Joey. I was sucking on a Tootsie Roll Pop, which I did quite often, before and after my sexual education with Susan. I kept hoping Joey would stop looking at me and just play his drums. He managed to catch my glance, and smiled. Oh, no. Jeez, no. The guy I don't want to go out with just caught my eye. Shit.

After the encore, and the usual wait time while some of the band members showered, Susan and Steven told me they had a surprise for me. Joey emerged from a small room, freshly showered and said hello. Steven and Susan said, "Nancy this is Joey. Joey this is Nancy."

9

We walked out of the dressing rooms and were escorted to the underground parking. Steven said to Joey and me, "Here, you kids take my car for the night." He was giving us his limo for the ride back to the hotel.

Joey and I got in the backseat of the limo. He was wearing a huge fur coat and twitching, a lot. His long hair was still wet from the shower. He had big lamb chops of hair growing on the sides of his face. He kept clearing his throat and speaking in an unnaturally high pitched voice. I found it difficult to look at him because I knew he "liked" me and I didn't like him. I'd get through this, I thought. I'm doing something nice for someone, I told myself.

It was a five minute ride to the Holiday Inn, Downtown Baltimore. Thank goodness. We went into the bar on the first floor. Joey asked a waiter for a table in the back where we could talk and hear ourselves think. Heading to the table, someone complimented Joey on the show. He genuinely thanked the person for the compliment. We sat down, ordered drinks and Joey began to tell me about his family.

I had never looked in his eyes until that moment. They were a piercing blue and they looked deeply into mine. I listened and looked back into his eyes as he told me about his three sisters, Annabelle, Amy and Suzy, his Mom, Dad and dog Tiger.

What's happening here? This long haired rock and roll guy is telling me about the things that matter most to him and I'm finding myself really enjoying his heartfelt stories and love for his family. What?

He was so happy and certain that I would like him if I just listened. I did. He asked if he could call me sometime and I said yes. I liked him.

I especially liked him for his honesty. He explained to me that with touring and being on the road so much, in order to date, I'd have to meet him on the road. Would I be willing to do that? He also said that he would respect my wishes regarding sexual intimacy and would get a separate room for me if I wanted. I was blown away by the proposal. How many rock and roll guys would do that?

Joey called a few days later and asked if I could come to Philadelphia for the show. It was October of 1974. He said to take the train, he'd pay for it. I could either take the train back or stay over and he'd get a second room. Wow. Nice. I liked being respected this way.

I stayed over, in his room, and he was true to his word; he made no advances.

Our next date was in Chicago. I flew this time, it was November, 1974. Joey rented a car and picked me up at the airport. He was dressed in a button down shirt and trousers. Oh my. The man really means business and cares what I think of him. Wow.

Joey had asked me on the phone before our second date how long I could stay. Being cute, I told him I'd stay one day for every Tootsie Roll Pop he had. When he opened the door to our hotel room there was a queen sized bed covered in blanket of Tootsie Roll Pops. Mr. Kramer had managed to surprise me and capture my heart in a most unusual and creative way. I stayed with him for three weeks and he was kind, sweet and made no advances.

Thanksgiving morning we woke up in Niagara Falls in a somewhat quaint motel. It was just before dawn. Joey sweetly and softly asked if we could make love. I said yes. Our worlds changed. I had never felt so loved, respected and beautiful as I did there with him. The sun came up and we went to see the beauty, power and magnificence of Niagara Falls. Oh my, I wasn't dreaming; we had fallen deeply in love.

Track 3

LITTLE BLACK BOOK – Sweet Surrender

I returned to Baltimore before Christmas and Joey continued touring with the band. I was in school, had a job and an already established plan to transfer to Boston College to study psychology and philosophy before I started dating Joey.

The year (1974) was coming to an end and something unexpected had happened. I didn't plan on falling in love with a guy I'd had a drink with after caving in under my friends' pressure. But I had, and to make matters worse, Joey called me a lot from the road and we had insightful conversations. Neither one of us spoke much about love or what had happened in Niagara Falls. Unbeknownst to him, he had found my weakness in matters of the heart; a quick wit and an intelligent mind. He worked his way deep into my heart and mind and he was quickly becoming a best friend, soul mate, everything good wrapped up in one small package.

Toward the end of December, Joey called and told me that the band would be off for a few weeks in January. He asked if I would come to Boston and spend New Years' Eve with him. Of course I would!

Joey picked me up at Logan Airport in his LT 1, 1971, Corvette. It was a gorgeous deep, yet intense bright blue color, with a black leather interior. It made impressive sounds and it scared me.

He was excited to see me and proud to show me the car that he had recently purchased. He said Joe Perry (lead guitarist for the band) had one like it. It was a monster of a car and pretty to look at. I didn't understand everything he tried to tell me about its mechanical workings and what made it so special, but I listened intently as he shifted gears darting in and out of traffic on the way to his apartment in Brighton, Massachusetts.

We were headed to Tremont Towers, a mid-rise building on Tremont Street, where Joey shared a two bedroom, one bath apartment with Mr. Saturday Night Fever, Steve Storlazzi. Joey described Storlazzi as a tough, little Italian who was "hot" with the chicks. Joey said Steve was also a great mechanic, his mechanic, of course. Joey told me I would also get to meet Tiger, his Great Dane who stood waist tall to him.

I was frightened by the thought of meeting a large dog; I still had a scar, a dime sized divot, on my buttocks where a German Shepard had taken a liking to me. I had teased the hell out of this dog chained to a tree with a black chiffon scarf that belonged to my mother. I was six and we still lived in Miami. We'd stopped by my grandfathers' bar so Mom could cash her paycheck and my brother and I were told to wait in the car. I got bored so I took the scarf sitting on the car seat where Mom had been and stepped outside the car to play. I saw King, the huge German Shepard, chained to the tree, behind my grandpa's bar. I started waving the scarf like a matador at the dog knowing he could only chase me so far because the chain and rope attached to his neck stopped him from reaching me. I was having a blast until the chain broke and King chased me all the way to the car. He was now free and came for me with a vengeance. To my horror and surprise he didn't stop until he reached his target. One chomp was all it took to tear through play shorts and panties leaving the scar on my butt.

I didn't want to meet Tiger, but Joey said it would be okay.

"Just don't tease him. He's well trained", Joey assured me. "If he really bothers you, I'll take him over to stay with a friend while you're here."

Okay, one fear down and none to go, I naively thought. I was now starting to enjoy the ride in his Corvette; moving fast, zipping in and around all the other cars on the expressway. Joey slowed down and got onto Storrow Drive which runs alongside the Charles River in Boston. I welcomed the slower pace of the scenic two lane artery leading into Beantown. Joey pointed out the town of Cambridge that was across the river and a few other points of interest along the way.

As we neared our destination Joey told me something that I'll never forget. He said he had called every girl in his "Little Black Book" and told them he was off the market. He said he informed every girl he used to date that he wouldn't be calling them anymore because he had met someone special.

I remember looking at the profile of his face while he was driving and thinking, "Wait. You can't do that. I don't like all that hair growing on the sides of your face!" Joey proudly wore long, wider than Elvis lamb chop sideburns in the early seventies.

"How could you do that?" I thought. In my mind, this was only our fourth or fifth date. I didn't even feel like I had seen his whole face yet!

So I asked him, "What's up with those things growing on your face?"

He told me he had a bad scar from being hit with a broken beer bottle while playing his drums at a college gig and had grown the hair to cover it.

Sweet Mother of God, he was working his way deeper into my heart. Second weakness in matters of the heart for me is a really good story about a really good scar. I told him that I'd love to see his entire face sometime.

We were almost parked when he told me about his finances. I didn't know why this was important to him until I realized that I made more money than him. I grossed $400 a week including tips and he received a regular paycheck of $250. Okay, so I didn't love him for his money and best I could tell his band wasn't going to provide him with much more than that; but he had my heart and a steady job.

Tiger, Joey's Great Dane, was at the door when we went into the small apartment and he was eager to get out. I freaked and Joey promptly took him to visit his friend, Nina.

Steve Storlazzi was exactly as Joey described; small, loud, wearing very tight fitting fuchsia colored pants and big collared black shirt, gold chains and an oversized gold cross around his neck. He was obviously annoyed by my presence; he seemed to idolize Joey and rudely competed with me for his attention.

Joey had the smaller bedroom. In it sat a queen-sized bed which pretty much went wall to wall and rested frameless, on the floor. It had red satin sheets and a leopard like fur covering the top. Where was I? I'd never seen any of these things before.

Joey said I could have the left side of the bed, the right side was his. I didn't know what a man cave was, but I was pretty sure I was in one.

The bathroom wasn't that bad for two guys living together; I could smell the remains of bleach when I made use of it. He must have tidied up for me and I appreciated the extra effort he took to make my visit comfortable.

It was New Year's Eve, 1974, and we were all set to have a fabulous time, staying in. We had carryout food, a bottle of champagne and each other's company. Mostly Joey talked and I listened. He told me so many stories that night: stories of the band, his family, past girlfriends, best friends in New York and one who lived out west. He talked endlessly about drumming, what it meant to him to be the best and his hope for his fathers' forgiveness one day. He talked about dropping out of Berkley School of Music in Boston due to an illness, his previous heroin use, and how much he wanted to please his parents.

I think he intended to serenade me that night with an old wooden guitar he'd brought out from the bedroom. We were sitting on the couch in the living room when he tuned the old guitar. A few minutes later, he leaned forward and promptly passed out, on top of the guitar.

I left him there in the living room and went to sleep in the bedroom. Hours later, I woke up to see him standing in the bedroom doorway. It looked as if he were holding up the door frame with his powerful biceps extended from side to side of the frame. He was clean shaven. He had an honest face with a scared look on it.

"I love you," he said. Then he repeated it as if I hadn't heard him the first time, "I love you." He came to bed, held me close, and went to sleep.

I told Joey when we woke up, the next day, New Years' Day 1975, that I had to think about getting back to Baltimore. I had things to wrap up at school in order to transfer to Boston College and money to make for an apartment in Boston. I did not tell him that I loved him too, until a few weeks later, when he asked. I was scared to confess my love for him; afraid that loving him might take me off track. I stayed for only a few days more and then went home to my job and my life in Baltimore. We continued to talk on the phone and I could feel myself getting closer and closer to him.

The weekend of my admissions interview at Boston College, Joey told me he would be out of town so I arranged to stay with a friend of Susan's in Boston. I had transcripts and a letter of recommendation from the Dean of the community college I attended in Essex, Maryland, in hand, as I flew into Boston on a Friday morning. I was wearing the lucky dress my Mama Maude (maternal grandmother) had bought me for my high school graduation, only eighteen months before. The slightly, longer than most, mini-dress, was powder blue with long sleeves that were cuffed at each end in white. Each cuff had one tiny red appliquéd strawberry where a cuff link would normally go. The matching white collar also had a strawberry appliqué on each long point. It was conservatively pretty, well fitted and saved for special occasions such as this.

Coming down the stairs at Logan Airport, I slipped on a piece of trash negligently left on a step, midway down the long, wide staircase and fell, bouncing on my rear all the way down. It would have been funny had I not broken my tail bone.

The pain was excruciating. Without cell phones and unable to get up, I began to cry. Hard. How would I get to my admissions interview? I knew I needed medical attention, but I was more concerned about getting to Boston College and keeping the long awaited appointment. Susan's friend had agreed to pick me up at the airport and drive me to the interview. We were to meet at Baggage Claim, and I couldn't get up.

A few kind strangers stopped to help and bombarded me with questions: Was I hurt? Could I get up? Where was I going? Did I need an ambulance? Shouldn't I file a report? What happened? And finally, did I have a lawyer?

I was crying so hard I couldn't get any words to come out of my mouth. I began to shake with uncontrollable emotion and horrendous pain at the tip of my spine. It was a bring-you-to-your-knees and squeeze the life out of you pain.

What I couldn't tell anyone trying to help me was that I knew the circumstances were ideal for a person with epilepsy to start seizing, right there at the bottom of the marble stairs at Logan Airport. Having been diagnosed and stigmatized with the condition of epilepsy following a grand mal seizure three years earlier while still in high school, I was at extreme high risk of having a grand mal seizure now and I knew it. I did not want to pass out and have uncontrollable convulsions on the hard stone stairs at Logan Airport.

Trying to deal with the pain and calm myself was the best option; adrenalin was now flowing and limb rigidity was easing. I kept breathing and focusing on just getting up, one breath and one step at a time. I dried my tears and asked the one person who had remained with me, if he would help me to get up, get my luggage and find a cab. He was a medical student in Boston and I was grateful that he'd extended himself to me.

He suggested that I go to my friend's apartment, call the college to reschedule the appointment and rest for the remainder of the weekend. He also said I'd be wise to invest in a child's inner tube pillow or inflatable donut to sit on. He told me if it still hurt Monday, I could be sure it was broken and to get an x-ray.

I cried in the cab, cried in the apartment and cried on the phone with someone from Admissions when they suggested that I wait until the following year to apply. I returned to Baltimore, defeated, and sat on an inflatable pillow with a hole in it for a week. My tail bone was broken and it would take weeks for it to heal. My soul was also

18

shattered from broken dreams I'd once held of attending a four-year university program in Boston.

Joey convinced me to fly back to Boston on January 15, 1975, to begin looking for an apartment. He said I could still keep my plan to move to Boston and work out the school part later. He said apartments didn't come easily in Boston and it might take a while to find exactly what I was looking for. When I arrived, still only able to sit on my pillow, Joey told me that he would be off, for the most part, until March, and why didn't I consider moving to Boston a little earlier than I'd planned. He said I could stay with him and we could spend time together while I searched for an apartment and he finished an album.

I was easily convinced. I loved him too. I wanted to be with him. I had a new version of an old dream; I imagined myself living as a single young woman in a darling Boston apartment, dating Joey and working for Playboy. And, having the good financial sense of my father, I'd be able to save more money if I worked for a longer period of time before returning to school as a fulltime student.

With my college dream resurrected, I flew back to Baltimore, packed up my car and moved 400 miles to Boston, Massachusetts.

Joey packed up Tiger and gave him away. Everything seemed perfect; we were really getting to know, love and trust each other. Being with him was fun, special, and an intimacy like I'd never known. And, he was crazy about me. He was crazy enough to want to be with me and only me, give away his dog and tear up his little black book. I truly believe he had my best interest at heart. He wanted me to be a Playboy Bunny, go to school and whatever else I dreamed of being.

I may have withheld telling him I loved him too for a few weeks, but on Valentine's Day, I baked him a chocolate cake with chocolate icing and wrote, "I Love You, Joey" on the top.

I had promised a friend from Baltimore, Phil Collector, that when I got to Boston, I'd call Erhard Seminars Training (EST) and go to an introduction about their training. Joey was away the night I was scheduled to attend "A Special Evening About the EST Training."

I invited Scott Melnick to go with me. I'd met Scott in the summer of 1973, when Susan and I went to Boston for the first time. He was a prissy, long haired Joe Perry (Aerosmith lead guitarist/songwriter) look-a-like who now lived in an old apartment where Joe Perry had once lived. He said he knew Joe and that they had worked together on cars. He didn't impress me much, but he was cute. That weekend, in the summer of 1973, when Susan and I were staying with a guitarist named Jimmy that Susan knew, Susan encouraged me to stay with Scott at his place so she could have Jimmy's loft apartment to herself.

I stayed the night with Scott, listening to him go on about Joe Perry, his cats with fleas, and his recent break-up with a longtime girlfriend. It was a long flea bitten night and neither one of us were interested in having sex.

Unlike me, a recent transport from Baltimore, Scott had lived in Boston all his life and knew his way around the city. I thought he would be the perfect person to escort me to the EST training introduction. He picked me up at Joey's about 7:00 p.m. He was very inquisitive about Joey, where he was, what was happening with the band and my relationship with him. As we opened the door to leave for the seminar, there was Joey. He had finished his work in NY early and raced home to surprise me. I was so happy to see him that I considered not going to seminar.

Joey was gracious and accepting of the fact that I had made plans. He told us to go ahead and said he'd be waiting for me when I got back. I was torn but remembered my promise to Phil and went to the EST introduction. Scott was bored with the presentation, thought it was a joke, a cult, and that he knew everything they were talking about already. He told me he wanted to leave and I said okay. I had fulfilled my promise to Phil to attend, so I convinced myself that I was free to leave.

Scott said it was early and asked if I had to get home right away. I told him I had a few minutes but was excited to get back and see Joey. I knew it was special that he had driven home early to surprise me. Scott drove to a newly erected high-rise apartment building and parked the car. It was dark. He began to tell me about building codes and how the builder of this complex had violated code and that the building was sure to fall down. I was 19 and so gullible. As I was trying to see the building in the dark and imagine what he was telling me, he reached over and tried to plant a French kiss on my mouth. I didn't see it coming and I was shocked and confused. I didn't want to be rude or offend him but I knew this wasn't right.

I had been raped two years earlier, by someone I knew, and I had a very hard time after that, speaking up for myself when placed in a compromising position like the one I was now in. I was scared, hurt and sad.

I told Scott I wasn't feeling well and asked if he could please take me home. He did and by the time we reached Joey's apartment I was physically ill. I made a bee line for the bathroom and threw up, just like I did after the rape.

Joey was concerned and compassionate when he came to the bathroom door to check on me. I told him I'd be out shortly. I knew I could trust him. I washed my face, brushed my teeth and made my way to bed. Joey held me close and asked about Scott. I told him that he had tried to kiss me and about the rape. It was difficult for me to talk about it; feeling so nauseous and recounting the experience to Joey, but for the first time in my life, I felt that here was a man who would fight for me and defend me if necessary. I was relieved to have shared the ugly tainted burden of the violent perpetration with someone worthy of my trust.

Joey made frequent trips to NY to finish the album, leaving me alone much of the time on Tremont Street. I interviewed with Playboy and was told that they wouldn't be hiring until mid March and that they would call me back for a second interview. I filled my time, waiting to hear back from Playboy, reading the classified ads for apartments and deep cleaning the former bachelor pad.

It would be at least another four to six weeks before my job with Playboy would begin, if I was hired. I missed my mom and my friends from home; Joey was gone more than he expected. My two best friends from Baltimore drove up to see me and I didn't realize just how homesick I was until I saw them. They came for a weekend in Jill's Chevy Vega with the car packed to the roof with the rest of my belongings. They were so excited to see me and visit Boston. We had an excellent weekend and I hated to see them leave.

After their visit, Joey had to leave again. It couldn't be helped; he had things to do with the band but should be back in a week. I was so sad when I walked him to the elevator to say goodbye. He held the elevator door open, kissed me and told me to get a job.

"Any job" he said. "Don't wait for Playboy to call you back, go find a job." I promised him that I would and found one that very same day.

The "Up and Up" rooftop lounge was inside of a hotel in Kenmore Square. They hired me to be a bartender. The manager who interviewed me knew I had no bartending experience but said he was impressed with my high achieving resume. He gave me a copy of the "Old Mr. Boston" Book of Bartending and told me to come back in two days to start work. I was thrilled.

It was a posh club overlooking the Charles River. The dark décor was plush with an abundance of comfortable, intimate seating, and the room was well lit with colorful, soft lighting. You could see the bright city lights of Boston from anywhere in the room. The live entertainment was upbeat and never failed to rhythmically move the guests to get up and boogie on the dance floor. I was having a blast in my newfound career of making cocktails. I enjoyed the music, the patrons, and the speed required to keep up with making drinks. I was glad to be making great money again and happy to be back on track with my goal of saving money for college.

A few weeks later, Joey called me at work to tell me that Judith, Bunny Mother at the Playboy Club, had called and wanted me to call her back. He said he had given her my work number and told her it would be okay to call me there.

Before I could even fully process what Joey had said, Judith called again. She asked me if I could come in the next day for a second interview. I told my manager at the Up and Up Lounge about the call from Judith and that I might be hired to be a Playboy Bunny. He said he was happy for me and that he knew when he hired me that I wouldn't be there for long.

I went for a total of seven interviews at the Playboy Club and it wasn't until the last interview that they put me in a Bunny costume to see what I looked like. Prior to that there were written tests, lots of questions and hypothetical what ifs to be intelligently answered by the applicant. Finally, I was put in the Playboy Bunny costume and asked to just walk across the floor to see whether or not I could be graceful, confident and beautiful while walking in those high heeled, pointed toed shoes.

I passed the final test and I was off to two weeks of Bunny Bootcamp. I knew about bootcamp training from my dad who had been in the US National Army Reserves. He went for two weeks of training every summer and he instilled in me the importance of training well to get a job done right. I took the training seriously and did my best to be a shining example of the honor it was to wear the uniform and represent Playboy Clubs of America.

A Playboy Bunny is a waitress, hostess or MC that works in the Playboy Club, wearing the coveted Playboy Bunny costume. A Playboy Playmate is someone chosen by Playboy, Bunny or not, and featured in a pictorial spread in Playboy Magazine.

Bootcamp was tough, there were daily written tests taken directly from the information found in the three training manuals that you were required to memorize and be able to recite at any given moment.

I was a young Bunny in the "hutch" of 43 girls. At 19, I may have been the youngest Bunny in the Boston Club, even though I seemed to have a maturity beyond my years. I was the newest Bunny to join the hutch for sure, and the older girls were very kind to me. They wanted me to succeed, partly for selfish reasons because the sooner I was well trained, the faster I could replace them at a last minute's notice to cover their shifts. Those girls really knew how to have last minute fun.

The Bunnies in the Boston Club and our Bunny Mother, Judith Morris, had a soft spot for me because not only was I young and new to Boston, but they sensed I missed my family and friends very much, and, to make matters worse, I had a boyfriend whose job took him away from me most of the time.

Back then I earned what would be the equivalent now of about $400 a day, working three to four shifts a week at Playboy. I found a sense of belonging with the girls in the Club. Whatever we were outside of the Club, law students, medical students, former waitresses and me, the girlfriend of a would-be-rockstar and a college student determined to graduate, in the Club we were all Bunnies in the hutch. We had the respect and attention of all who entered. We were treated like stars and had our own private entrance and elevator to our large, shared, dressing room. We had a fulltime seamstress to launder and care for our costumes, provide us with the regulated Playboy pantyhose that would later be deducted from our paychecks and help us dress before our shift. This kind, older woman, with a constant smile and heavy German accent also listened quietly to our little woes and worries on any given day. She had a long tool that she used to zipper the tight fitting Playboy costume up the back while we sucked in, held our breath and our waists with both hands, so she could zipper the thing all the way up! It took an hour to get ready, start to finish. Before going on the floor for work, you had to go to the Bunny Mother's office for inspection. Like a good mother, the Bunny Mother checked everything. With an Admiral's scrutiny, she looked at us from head to toe for polished, un-scuffed shoes, two pairs of pantyhose (one beige support pair underneath a second pair of Playboy jet black hose), a clean white fluffy Bunny tail hooked securely on, well manicured nails, stuffing in the bust of the costume (no matter how well endowed you might be), full make-up including the mandatory wearing of false, strip eyelashes, Bunny ears cutely curving in just the right way, starched white collar and straight black bowtie, and lastly, starched white cuffs with the Playboy cufflinks "kissing" when you crossed your wrists in front of her. With her approval and cheerleading words to you, off you went to be a Playboy Bunny!

As stated in the official Playboy Bunny manual, you were expected to maintain your "Bunny Image" everywhere you went.

Always in make-up, never with curlers in your hair to the grocery store, or anywhere else you may happen to wander. We had agreed to these conditions when we signed on to be Playboy Bunnies. I took it seriously and had a real sense of belonging to something great. Playboy had Clubs all over the world, an extremely popular magazine and I was, naturally, loyal to the brand. In exchange, the people in the Club treated us like celebrities. Walking through the club always reminded me of films I'd seen about the US Navy. When we passed by, it was as if someone had yelled, "ATTENTION: Officer on Deck!" You didn't have to ask for the attention, it was freely given.

All Bunnies started with one new, custom fitted costume and Playboy management chose the color for you. You had to write your name on your white cotton tail to be sure it could be counted and come back to you after being laundered. You were forbidden to take your costume out of the Club. Only time and good behavior would earn you a second costume, in a color of your choosing. The coveted black Playboy Bunny costume was reserved for those Bunnies who had achieved "Penthouse" status. I remember only two such Bunnies in my Club. The "Penthouse" was where the big name entertainers would come in for sold-out shows and to be a Bunny in the Penthouse required additional training. You had to learn to speak before the show to the crowd and introduce the talent that would be performing that night. You were guaranteed four times as much money for those shifts than you would have received working on any other level of the Club. Other than being chosen for a layout or cover in the Playboy Magazine, this was one of the highest honors you could achieve.

Another special assignment was being trained to sit in for the Bunny Mother, from time to time. All of these girls, in both circumstances, had to be strong and well seasoned to handle the job. I never worked the Penthouse or sat in for Judith, our Bunny Mother. Three of the girls in my Club were sisters and had been there a long time. They seemed to be favored with prime shifts and some of the Bunny Mothers' responsibilities; they'd earned it.

Carol, also a newbie but older than me, took me to her apartment one afternoon and tweezed my bushy brother eyebrows to a thin

Lucille Ball shape. It was painful and afterwards I had to tweeze them twice a day to maintain the shape.

I think it was Monika Z and Suzy K who had been there the longest. Monika was off on Saturdays and Suzy worked mostly lunches. They had earned their privileged schedules and black costumes; I admired them both. Suzy's former husband, Brad, was a hair stylist, and at her suggestion, I made an appointment for my first salon haircut. Brad worked in a small hip salon on Newberry Street and gave me long, sexy bangs with my new cut. I think both Alexis R and Suki V had my favorite color costume, a brilliant canary yellow. Suki also had a beautiful turquoise costume. The Clubs' choice for me was tangerine orange, and it was okay, but I really wanted canary yellow or turquoise.

Playboy Bunnies were also required to do goodwill volunteer service in the community; answering phones live on TV for the Jerry Lewis Telethon each year for Muscular Dystrophy, supporting the Dairy Association by milking cows in Boston Commons, riding in Fourth of July Parades in a jeep with servicemen from America's Armed Forces and collecting donations for underprivileged kids at Patriot's home football games.

It may sound silly, but Playboy had a policy of giving back to the community, not just building the brand. I enjoyed every aspect of being a Playboy Bunny and volunteered often. I was proud to have been chosen to represent the iconic American brand.

Hugh Hefner's daughter trained in our Club as a Playboy Bunny, learning the enterprise from the ground up. I admired the fact that she was not given special treatment or special privileges; she was just one of us.

One day in late February 1975, after Playboy boot camp and before I officially began working in the Club, Joey offered to drive me to see the one-bedroom apartments I had circled in the newspaper. The first one was listed as a studio apartment on Beacon Street, near Back Bay in Boston. It was a walk down space that looked like a basketball court and was about half the size of an NBA court. No kitchen, no bathroom, no plumbing. I was so disappointed, the ad had sounded great.

Fighting back tears, I jokingly asked Joey if he liked to play basketball. The only thing missing in this room was a ball; clearly it wasn't suitable for anything else.

Joey laughed as I tried to hide my tears and then a slow, warm smile came over his face and he asked me in a very soft voice, "Nan, would you consider sharing an apartment with – me?"

No, I hadn't thought of that; it didn't fit the picture in my mind of living as a single woman in Boston in a darling apartment and dating Joey. My heart began to flutter as the warmth and sincerity of his words rushed over me.

I had been white-lying to my family and former high school boyfriend, John Newman, about who I was staying with in Boston. I told them I was staying with "Joie Kramer," a girl I'd met through Susan, in Baltimore. It was easier for me to say this than to acknowledge that I was really living with Joey, now warrior and defender of my heart. My mail came to Joey's apartment addressed to:

Nancy Karlson

C/O (in care of) Joie Kramer

121 Tremont Street

Brighton, MA 02135

Where I came from, you didn't "shack up." It was considered to be taboo and you were unholy if you did.

So here I stood, on the court, inside a huge unusable room for rent on Beacon Street, with Joey asking me to officially share a home with him for the entire world to see. As I stood there, engulfed by his sweetness, cheeks flushing and eyes tearing, I told him I'd need to think about it and he told me to take all the time I needed. To me, he now looked like the man, the joyful wizard behind the curtain in Oz. He was obviously excited, like a child in anticipation of getting what he wants for Christmas. It made me smile.

The next few days were blissful and Joey was on his best princely behavior. We both knew I'd say yes, my old morals just had to catch up to my new morality. Our committed relationship had officially begun.

Once again I searched the newspapers, but this time for the place where we'd make our home, together. I found an adorable attic apartment inside of a huge old house on Waban Street in Newton, MA. It was in the suburbs, a perfectly respectable abode for a newly, exclusively committed couple, living together.

My whole world shifted when we moved in together. All of the secret longings I had for marriage and children, all the things I'd carefully placed in my hope chest upon high school graduation less than two years before, were now within reach of becoming a reality. I wanted it all; love, marriage, a college degree and children.

I made a fine little nest for us, in about 600 square feet. The entrance was in the back of the house and you walked up three wooden fights of stairs to enter our front door. Then you walked up another flight of carpeted stairs to our little loft of an apartment. Straight ahead was a walk-in closet pretending to be a small bedroom and to the right was an 8x10 living room. Next was a 10x12 kitchen, with a very small bathroom off to the right, and lastly, the biggest room in the apartment, our bedroom. It held our king size bed, a couple of dressers and night stands, one comfortably sized long closet for two and a little dressing nook where I put an antique vanity table with mirror. It was Joey's idea to buy me a vanity table and he picked it out. He purchased it for $40 and set it up for me in the small, low ceiling corner of the room. This is where I would get ready with hair and make-up. The wooden vanity table was made of a dark wood that had aged to be almost black in color. The mirror was dark and cloudy. It had four tiny little drawers to hold make-up, perfume, brushes and clips for one's beautification. You could still smell the cosmetic sweetness of my predecessors. My hair curlers were so big they wouldn't fit in the drawers so I kept them on the top of the table and my portable, hooded-sit-while-you-dry hair dryer, underneath. Joey loved to watch me sit there and do my girly things.

He was always smiling, always attentive, in those first few months. We went to Chestnut Hill Mall and Joey sprang for two sets of satin sheets, one pink set and one baby blue set for our new king size bed to put them on. We bought pots and pans, knick knacks and framed pictures for the seven and a half foot walls. I made curtains on my sewing machine and hung them on the three small windows in our apartment. We built a pantry for food from steel shelving and I made curtains for that too and draped them over the front of the shelving unit so you couldn't see the food it housed.

We had two parking spaces in the back of the house, a rare find in the Boston area, which we didn't have to pay for. Joey parked his blue Vet there and I parked my still Maryland tagged 1973 white and turquoise blue vinyl topped Datsun coupe.

It was cold outside when we moved in and Joey felt that I didn't have a warm enough winter coat or suitable boots for the long lasting winter in Boston, so he gave me $100 and sent me back to Chestnut Hill Mall to buy a coat and boots. I spent a considerable amount of time shopping for them (after a quick visit to the cosmetic counter) and came home with a rust colored leather jacket and high heeled boots to match. The jacket was fitted, no buttons, zippers or snaps, just wrapped and tied at the waist. It had a five inch wide natural lamb's wool collar that you could flip up and have it almost touch your ears. I thought it was perfect and that I would be adequately covered and protected from cold weather of any kind. And it was so darn cute with those matching rust colored high heeled leather boots.

When I got home from the mall and tried them on for Joey, all he could do was laugh. He said, "What did you buy? This is gonna take you through the rest of winter?"

Still laughing, he said, "Keep them. I'll get you a winter coat."

Sure enough, he came home from the next band tour with one that would have kept me warm in Alaska. The rust colored sheepskin coat was four inches thick with a collar that flipped up, more than covering my ears. Equipped with buttons, hooks and a wide leather belt that tied at the waist, it covered both butt and thighs. Whatever a New England winter may bring, I was now ready.

One not so cold Sunday morning, Joey took me out for my first ever bagel from a Bagel Shop, and I was able to don the cute set of boots and jacket that I had chosen from the mall. Joey was tickled with how I looked in them and that I had naively thought they'd carry me through winter. He ordered two bagels with lox, cream cheese, onion and tomato, lightly toasted. I'd never tasted anything so good. In my home growing up, Mom occasionally baked small frozen mini bagels in the oven and served them with a Sunday meal, pretending that they were dinner rolls. No condiments were offered other than soft butter. I had no idea what a real, over-sized New York Jewish style bagel was; mighty tasty when properly garnished.

Joey enjoyed introducing me to so many firsts in my lifetime. He was especially excited to take me to New York to meet his parents, Mickey and Doris, and his three younger sisters, Annabelle, Amy and Suzy. He'd been bragging to them about the nice girl he'd met from Baltimore and he told them of the home we'd made in Newton. They too, looked forward to meeting me; the young woman who seemed to have made so many changes for the better in their only son and big brother.

We flew to New York from Boston on March 1, 1975 for a visit with them in their home in White Plains. Joey's mom greeted us with open arms and told me shortly after we arrived that she was old-fashioned and I'd be sleeping in young sister Suzy's room. She said that even though she knew we were living together and sharing a bed in Boston, under her roof, we would not sleep in the same room. She was right to do so; she had three young impressionable daughters.

They had a cozy cot set up for me in Suzy's room. Young, adorable Suzy and I liked each other from the start. The older girls, Annabelle and Amy were more cautious than curious about who their brother was dating. I would later learn that I was not Joey's first, live-in girlfriend and that they had been close to his former girlfriend, Nina.

Joey's dad, Mickey, was a hoot. Cigar smoking, joke cracking funny, he was a big dimpled salesman who owned his own advertising company in the city, "Jumbo Advertising." He seemed to always be selling something to somebody. He loved to sit in his easy chair with his feet propped up on an ottoman in their family room after driving home from a long day's work. He would sit comfortably and smoke his small cigar, rattle the ice in his drink and chat with anyone who entered the room while waiting for his wife Doris to get the evening meal on the table. I was sold on the warmth and traditions that he and his family were offering; they were very kind to me and treated Joey and I like an engaged to be married couple.

Joey's mom, Doris, worked in community theatre and couldn't wait to show me her talent of tap dancing, shoes and all, while cooking dinner. She had a naturally loud, live stage voice and everyone listened when she spoke. If not, she could get really loud. She too, had really cute dimples and a smile that could light your way out of a forest. Her hair was short, spiked and frosted. She had piercing green hazel eyes and wore a lot of Maybelline black eyeliner – top, bottom and inside the lower eye rim. Doris, like Mickey, was playful and jovial, but ran a very tight ship inside her home. You didn't dare mess with her.

Joey and I were in the kitchen with her when she encouraged Joey to go into the family room where Mickey was relaxing and listening to an album of Frank Sinatra. Doris insisted that Joey go into the family room and just talk to his father. Joey solemnly returned to the kitchen a few minutes later. I remember Doris telling him, "Well, one day. You've just got to keep trying."

I didn't understand everything about Joey's troubled relationship with his dad. I only knew that Joey was guilt ridden for having left college, used drugs and gotten sick (hepatitis) for an extended period of time. He told me that he felt like he was a huge disappointment to his father and no "just talking" to him would make things right. It was uncomfortable to be around the two of them. They didn't speak, even when in the same room. No forgiveness seemed in sight. Joey was hurt to the core.

Doris suggested that I drive Suzy somewhere across town to pick up something. I don't remember what, but it was an honor to have the trust of Doris to drive her youngest child, anywhere. I assumed that she wanted us out of the house so she could help to orchestrate peace between her son and his father.

While in the car, Joey's band's song, "Dream On," came on the radio and Suzy wanted to know what the song was about. I was more than impressed that this tender young mind would ask such a question. I did my best, very best, verse by verse, to lend my interpretation of the song and its relevant meaning to aging, going through life and being kind to others. Suzy was satisfied with my answer and suggested that maybe people should grow up to be whatever they wanted to be. She didn't understand the trouble between her father and brother, only that they weren't free to express any love or be themselves with each other. I remember wishing that her father, Mickey Kramer, had been in the car with us.

Joey and I returned to Boston on Tuesday, March 12, 1975, on the Eastern Airlines shuttle. On March 22, 1975, I flew on a Delta flight to Baltimore and came clean with my mom about Joey. I was starting a new life and a new job and didn't want this lie hanging over me. I told my mother what she'd already guessed; I was living with Joey.

Joey was especially nervous those first few weeks in April, 1975, with the release of the album they'd been working on, "Toys in the Attic," and knowing that he was to play at two sold out concerts, April 18 & 19, at home. I don't know why it was always such a big deal for the band to play in Boston; I guess it was because it was their hometown and it's often harder to perform well before those you know and who have witnessed your success firsthand.

Joey was excited for me to see the band's popularity at home. He became overly nervous again when he found out that Laura Kaufman, PR Manager for the Band, would be flying up from New York for the show with a few people from the press. I was getting quite good at comforting his fears; I assured him that everything would be okay. I remember Joey telling me, "They want a solo. They want a drum solo performance from me. This is our hometown; it's expected."

I told him he would do a drum solo when he was ready and it didn't have to be at the Boston Garden. Joey liked the way I could help him make his fears disappear, naturally. Freed of the burden of "having to perform" a drum solo, Joey seemed to enjoy his own playing, both nights in Boston. I enjoyed the crowd's reaction to the band and seeing my drummer boy comfortable, confident and genuinely having a good time on stage. I was so damn happy for him. I wanted him to have the desires of his heart and first and foremost, I thought it was the band.

At the After Party, at the Orson Wells Cinema in Cambridge, Joey introduced me to a very busy Laura Kaufman, from Leber-Krebs Management, who was hosting the party. I was amazed at how easily and effortlessly this small but mighty native New Yorker was greeting everyone, like Emily Post on steroids. Laura graciously welcomed each and every invited guest with a smile, handshake and sincere good wishes for an enjoyable evening meeting the band. It was a well planned PR event and the band was expected to behave. In attendance were people from the press, hundreds of uniquely interesting looking people and their guests, each and every one invited for how they could potentially promote the band's success.

Laura had to keep track of the band members' whereabouts; she needed all hands on deck, but especially Steven's, for impromptu introductions and interviews. The Orson Wells Cinema had only two bathrooms as I remember, and Steven was in one and Joe Perry was in the other, for most of the night. They were, of course, doing what Rockstars did in the bathrooms, in the seventies: snorting Cocaine and inviting only those inside the bathroom who had more drugs to share. Laura had precision radar for Steven and Joe. She seemed to know where and with whom they were at all times; strongly allied with two reporting and indulgent field lieutenants in Bob Kelleher and Ray Tabano. Their paychecks were also signed by Leber-Krebs.

On May 24, 1975, I flew to Dayton, Ohio on TWA flight #511 with Terry Cohen, Aerosmith bass player Tom Hamilton's future wife. We flew down to meet the boys on the road – the Toys in the Attic Tour, 1975. It had been three weeks since any of us had had a conjugal visit and we were all due. This was the beginning of the three week pact that Joey and I made. We promised to not go more than three weeks without seeing each other; he would fly home or I would fly out to wherever he was. It was a way to manage normalcy in our relationship.

Terry and I, traveling together on this leg of the tour, began an intimate friendship. Terry, like Joey and everyone else I was surrounded by, was five years older and wiser than me. I began to look to my newly adopted family of Aerosmith and Playboy to teach me the things I didn't learn in the home I grew up in. My parents were regretful teenagers when they married and had me, and they had little interest in raising children. They divorced after two years and my mom, brother and I moved into my grandparent's home. For a short while, I experienced unconditional love and guidance from my maternal grandparents. Five years later, my teenaged parents remarried each other, as if they hadn't gotten it terribly wrong the first time. It was hell growing up in that home. Their second marriage lasted ten years mostly because my father was never home and my mom drank, heavily. I relied on school, church, sports and music to survive.

Terry was an artist, totally down to earth, honest and funny. She had that artist chic Bohemian approach to living. Tom and Terry had been living together for several years and both were grounded, easy to be around people. I admired them and was grateful for their friendship and willingness to share their ideas and life experiences with me. Their families had remained intact. To the best of my knowledge they had not suffered the consequences or shame of childhood neglect, abandonment, manipulation and the worst, sexual molestation. I wanted to get as far away from the painful memories of my past as I possibly could. I sought refuge in my relationship with them.

Terry wasn't overtly nurturing, by nature. She often would crack a good joke as a way of offering comfort to a bleeding soul. She was funny, in a sarcastic way, and knew just the right amount of Yiddish to make anything she said sound funnier. She wasn't a hugger or a kisser but you knew she cared just the same.

Terry Cohen also introduced me to many firsts and finer things. She taught me how to appreciate a really fine dark red wine, oysters on the half shell, ratatouille and good soulful music and reggae. She taught me proper pot etiquette and intelligent consumption of Quaaludes, 714. She demonstrated by example how to manage recreational drugs and enjoy a fine evening with dinner and great conversation. Terry always seemed to bring art to everything she did, and I liked that way of being.

Terry and I flew on with our guys to Fort Wayne, Indiana and Detroit, Michigan, for two sold out shows at Cobo Hall. Public relations for the band held an after party at the Detroit Playboy Club. Rock Scene magazine was on hand to photograph the band with the Bunnies and Joey was proud to tell them that his girlfriend was also a Playboy Bunny back home in Boston. I felt pretty dang special.

Terry and I left our guys in Detroit and flew back to Boston on the same flight. Sensing that I'd not yet grown a thick skin for saying goodbye, Terry suggested we have an in-flight drink.

"Have a cocktail…get a little looped on the flight," she told me.

"We'll be home before ya know it" she continued. "You'll come over, we'll do something fun." I was consoled and glad to have her as a friend in Boston. Terry understood first hand the pain of separation I felt with Joey. She missed Tom too but had gotten really good at filling her time in creative and fun ways. She had strong family ties with her family in Worcester, many longtime friends, and, of course, got on well with most of the people related to Aerosmith.

Terry loved hearing my work stories and what was going on inside the Playboy Club. Although it wasn't her thing, she seemed to be slightly impressed that I was a Bunny. I was happy that she cared and offered me genuine friendship. Terry and Tom's apartment on Beacon Street was always the preferred place to be when we'd get together to fight the boredom and loneliness of our boys being gone. We'd have a rough idea of how we'd spend our time together and usually it would include a light vegetarian meal that Terry would cook, a bottle of decent red wine and a little weed. Terry would always have one or two wooden easels with unfinished canvases set up in the dining room so we'd eat sitting on the floor at the coffee table in her living room. I could always judge her level of inspiration and creativity with her artwork as to whether or not I could smell fresh paint lingering and mingling with the spicy herbed vegetables cooking. If I smelled both, I knew we were in for a joyously creative evening a la Terry.

Terry didn't smoke cigarettes but would occasionally take a puff of mine if she was really excited. I always admired how she could have just one puff and walk away.

It was hard not seeing Joey and Tom for long periods of time; three weeks can seem like an eternity when it's a regular occurrence. We were the ones waiting at home for their return. Terry always made the time pass faster. Everything was an art form with her. Sometimes we'd just take a joyride in her 240Z Datsun listening to the Eagles, Fleetwood Mac and her favorite, Bob Marley. We'd often smoke a joint in her car while driving nowhere special which made her already low and sultry sexy voice seem even lower and slower. Terry had a thick Bostonian accent that I loved to listen to. Being with her took away much of the pain and isolation I felt in Joey's absence.

My long, curly blonde haired warrior, Joseph Michael Kramer, was the same height as me, 5'6", and born on the summer solstice in 1950. I learned to like and wear flat shoes, so that he would seem taller than me. He looked a lot like James Cagney and had soulful blue eyes that you could get lost in. He'd often call me from the road and teasingly say, "So-whatcha been up to?" This would often lead to, "So-whatcha wearing?" Joey named my biblical garden "Kitty" and his manly staff, "Willie." He'd ask me if Kitty was being a good girl and tell me that Willie missed her. It was long distance, PG rated phone sex and it, too, helped the time go by faster until I'd see him again.

Track 4

HOTEL CALIFORNIA –
Forgiving Fornications

On Friday morning, June 20, 1975, the day before Joey's 25th birthday, I was scheduled to work lunch at the Club. Joey was in LA, Aerosmith had played the Los Angeles Forum the night before. Even though Terry had been great company and I was busy at work, I missed Joey terribly. It was so close to his birthday, I felt compelled to call the hotel and offer him some of Kitty's sweetness. They were staying at the Beverly Hills Hotel and I knew I'd be waking him up. It was 10:00 a.m. in Boston and 7:00 a.m. in Los Angles. I could hardly wait for him to answer the phone so I could sweetly purr and tell him *Happy Almost Birthday, Kitty misses Willie!*

I had carefully planned to be ready for work with hair and make-up already done so I could spend 15-20 minutes with Joey on the phone before driving into Boston. I was sure to surprise him and I thought what a great early birthday present it would be to give my fella.

I dialed carefully, asked for his room and after many rings, a girl answered his phone. Confused and feeling my heart sink in my chest, I asked her if Joey was there. She said yes and then I heard her say, "Joey, wake up, it's for you."

I heard Joey reply in a very tired and groggy voice, "What?"

I heard the girl in his room, whom I'm sure I had also woken up, say, "Here, take the phone, it's for you."

Even 3,000 miles away, I could tell Joey's eyes were not yet open when he took the receiver and said, "Hello."

Somehow, managing to speak, I said, "Hi. It's me. I wanted to wish you a happy early birthday but I guess the surprise is on me."

Joey said, "Nan. It's not what you think, let me call you back."

"Don't bother. I'm on my way to work," I told him, as calmly as I could.

I got off the phone, shaking. I had to drive to work and I knew this was no time to let myself be upset. The phone rang. I picked it up and Joey said, "Nan, let me explain. It was a good time, that's all. Please don't be upset."

I hung up the phone again, a bit calmer this time, and drove to work.

By the grace of God, I did not cry all the tears in my heart before I got there. I knew I had to be strong to survive this and for the first time, I felt that maybe I might have my mother's Southern grit. About midway through the Friday lunch shift at the Club, a Western Union Telegram arrived and was delivered to me by the Floor Manager. It was from Beverly Hills, California and read:

> NAN I KNOW YOU'RE UPSET PLEASE DON'T BE
> I'M BORED AND LONELY WHAT I MEAN BY A GOOD
> TIME IS JUST THAT DON'T MISUNDERSTAND HAVE
> A GOOD WEEKEND ALL MY LOVE JOEY.

It had instructions on it to be delivered ASAP.

A few minutes later a dozen red roses were brought to me by Bunny Suzy, who was working in the lobby when they arrived. The card was signed, "All my love, Joey."

Everyone thought it was such a lovely romantic gesture and told me what a special guy I must have. I smiled, thanked them and prayed for the time to come quickly when I could leave and get the hell out of there.

Tears began to fall like a sudden summer rain as soon as the employee's entrance steel door banged shut behind me. The sound of that door closing marked the end for me of something I loved with all my heart; our fidelity. I cried all the way home and into the next day.

38

"HAVE A GOOD WEEKEND." How the hell was that possible? It was his birthday, I was alone, betrayed and waiting to answer a phone that didn't ring.

Our fidelity meant everything to me: it was a given in my book. He wanted me more than anyone, had made a gallant effort to capture and hold my heart. I thought he would protect and defend it, forever. It never occurred to me that he might find comfort in the arms of someone else.

I wondered what I'd say to him when he got back. One thing was for certain; it wouldn't be me picking him up at the airport to give him a ride home. I called no one, I told no one about how my weekend went. I was deeply hurt, ashamed and grieving a loss of innocence. This was the first time I'd ever been cheated on; I knew it happened, I'd watched it with my parents, but I never thought it would happen to me.

I couldn't tell anyone, not my parents, not my girlfriends from home, not even Terry. It seemed the only person I'd be able to talk to about it was Joey. In my lovely bubble of a world, this should never have happened and he was the only one who could make things right again.

I moved from hurt to anger when I thought about all the offers I'd had and never given a second thought. Boys from home wondering what the hell had happened to me sent messages to me through my mom. Men and cute boys were everywhere in Boston and, as I was faithfully maintaining my "Bunny Image", they noticed. I had offers all the time, especially around the Playboy Cub. Dating Key Holders (Playboy Club Members) was strictly prohibited at that time but the visiting professional athletes, entertainers, television stars and even the Club's General Manager, Gene Perkins, were all fair game.

They showed strong interest in me, as they would with any Bunny, but I never once looked back or encouraged any advances. I was in love with Joey from the tips of my toes to the top of my head; how could he possibly have done this?

Terry called me on Monday and said that Joey had told Tom what had happened. That was a good first step, I thought; I found it comforting to know that Tom and Terry were helping to shoulder the burden of my shame.

As I was making dinner, the phone rang again and it was Joey this time.

"Hello," he said. "Whatcha doin'?"

"Making dinner for one," I replied, doing my best to hold back the tears.

"Well, I'm gonna see ya in two weeks," he said with a smile in his voice.

"Really?" I had honestly forgotten that I was scheduled to fly to LA to be with him. In my mind, nothing would ever be the same and I was planning my escape from the pain that my heart could no longer hold.

"Yes, you're flying out with Lori (Brad's girlfriend). We put you both on the same flight. Lori has the tickets."

I said nothing.

Joey continued, "It's the first time to the west coast for both of you. She's really sweet, Nan. She'll pick you up and you gals come out together."

Still silence on my end. What could I say? What did I want? Could I trust that he really loved me and had made a stupid mistake?

"Nan, just get on the plane with Lori. We'll work everything out when you get here."

"They've made a big deal of us (Aerosmith) here in LA. I want you to see it, to experience it with me. From here we'll go on to Hawaii. Please come."

For a few seconds I couldn't respond. I could hear his voice but his words were drowned out by the louder pounding sound of my own heart racing with cutting disappointment and grief. I could barely breathe, my ears were ringing and I thought I might pass out before I could form any words.

"Nan, please, just get on the plane with Lori. I promise everything will be okay. I love you. I promise we'll get it all worked out when you get here."

I knew he loved me, with his whole heart, even though I didn't understand his behavior. I knew nothing of a set of rules, acceptable promiscuous behavior, for guys in bands while touring.

"Okay, I'll come."

"Good, I'll call you in a couple of days. I love you. Be good."

When Lori picked me up and gave me my airplane ticket I saw that it was issued to, "Mrs. J Kramer." Was that supposed to make me feel better? Was that intended to make me forget his transgressions and think that I was someone special, even forget his awful birthday blunder?

It did; somewhat. A guy doesn't call you Mrs. and put it on a plane ticket for all to see unless his intentions are honorable, right?

I got on the plane with Lori and flew to LA. It was a long, long flight.

Brad and Lori lived in Framingham, outside of Boston, more of a rural setting. Lori's whole world was framed around making herself a good wife-to-be for Brad. She knew about recipes, laundering tips, home furnishings and where to make reservations for dinner. Lori was a wistful bride in the making.

I don't remember much past my own deep, personal pain those first few days in LA. I do recall waking up, unable to open my eyes with conjunctivitis in both eyes, after the first night I spent back in Joey's arms.

Joey took me to the eye clinic at UCLA for treatment. I was happy to see a doctor and glad to be told to throw my eye make-up away and instructed not wear make-up for two weeks. I didn't want to be bothered with anything – especially being around people who knew what had happened on Joey's birthday.

We slept a lot, or at least pretended to. Neither one of us were experienced in how to deal with the truth of infidelity in the space of love and romance. We loved each other very much and respected the deep friendship bond between us.

Joey rented a car and we drove around LA, seeing the touristy spots and trying new foods at different restaurants. We ate a tremendous amount of leafy green vegetables and drank fruit protein shakes, almost daily.

We made a special trip to see the large billboard sign of the band on Sunset Boulevard – their faces larger than life, that Tower Records had put up.

We went to see a movie at the famous Grauman's Chinese Theater. I don't remember what we saw because I was so uncomfortable in the tight jeans I was wearing and the bad gas stomach pains in my belly from all the fresh foods and milk based protein shakes we'd consumed. Sitting next to Joey in the theater, I had no idea that the gas I was about to pass was as foul and vile as the feeling I was harboring about Joey and the girl who slept with him. I quietly began to let it go and to my horror it was the worst thing I'd ever smelled. I wanted to laugh with its release – but then I would be claiming it. I remained seated, silent and expressionless.

"What the fuck was that?" Joey uttered as he turned his head to look at the people in the row behind us.

"Jesus man, that smells horrible!" Looking at a large man seated in the row behind us, Joey continued, "Holy shit man, ya coulda gone outside to let that one go!"

Quiet as a church mouse, I laughed so hard, on the inside. A part of me felt totally justified that Joey should be subject to my internal stink.

After the movie we went to Tower Records to see how the new album was displayed and take in one of the world's largest record stores. While we were browsing the ridiculously long rows of albums, I felt another warm sensation in the seat of my pants and knew another – clear the theater – silent but deadly, obnoxious gas emission was coming. I slithered a few aisles over, away from Joey, thinking all would be well. Not a chance. From two aisles over I heard,

"Holy shit, Nan! That same guy from the theater is here! Jesus, do you smell that? It's the same rank smell. Let's get outta here!"

I was really roaring now (on the inside) although oblivious to Joey because he was too busy crucifying the wrong guy for being out in public. We got in the car and drove back to the hotel. I never did claim it and I smile to this day when I think about it.

On July 7, with our plane tickets issued to Joey Kramer and Mrs. Joey Kramer, we flew to Honolulu with the rest of the band for a show at the HIC Arena on July 13, 1975. We would have six days off before the show and Joey and I would spend part of our time, alone, on the island of Kauai.

Joey slept for most of the five and a half hour flight to Hawaii, while I sat next to him looking out the airplane window seeing nothing but deep, endless dark water. The sun was shining through the plane's window and I welcomed its warmth and Joey's soft, rhythmic breathing next to me. I tried to convince myself that we were leaving Los Angeles and its demons behind. I wanted to forgive him and be back on solid ground but the vast ocean kept reminding my heart how far away from Joey it now was. We still had not spoken of his birthday blunder and at 19, I wasn't yet equipped with great communication skills or knowledge of how to restore the integrity of a broken relationship. I was counting on him to lead the way and show me the art of forgiveness.

When we landed, everyone went their separate ways. As I remember, Joey and I stayed for one night in touristy Honolulu and then flew to Kauai the next day. Kauai was a small island, but famous for the Coconut Palms Hotel where Elvis Presley had filmed one of my favorite movies, "Blue Hawaii." I think Joey may have chosen this nostalgic and romantic setting for us as a place to begin healing what was broken between us. At least I wanted to think so.

Every evening, thong-skirted Hawaiians would run through the lush gardens with torches in hand and ceremoniously light gas burning lanterns. I recall wishing on one of those nights that a torch-bearing Hawaiian would come close enough to me that he could relight the flame in my heart for love. When I didn't feel the pain in my heart, I felt numb.

We were in one of the most beautiful places in the world with all of its sights, sounds and colors and I could barely manage to smile. We ate sumptuous meals by candlelight of fresh fish, fruits and desserts and sampled exotic island drinks. We strolled along white sand and black stone uninhabited beaches with beautiful flowers extending almost to the water's edge and I remained untouched, unable to taste, smell or see the beauty that surrounded me.

I can tell you the music I listened to because I'd recently purchased Simon & Garfunkel's cassette recording of "Bookends" and a small battery operated tape player. I listened to the songs on that album over and over again during our stay in Hawaii as if they were somehow saving my soul. It's not a particularly uplifting album but the songs lyrics seemed to massage my broken heart and provide hope that I would recover from Joey's betrayal and loss of my innocence.

We flew back to Honolulu for the show and retreated again afterwards for a few days at a hotel on the North Shore of Oahu.

The hotel had an upscale classic ladies clothing boutique and one night after dinner Joey and I went in to browse. I noticed a lovely white halter top and slinky bell bottom pants set that I thought was simply stunning. Other than smiling after farting in the famous theater in LA, this was the first time that I'd smiled in weeks. Joey asked if I wanted to try it on and I lied and told him I didn't like it that much. I felt justified in lying to him and protecting my heart because he hadn't asked for forgiveness yet. We never talked about what happened in LA or what to expect in the future in terms of our fidelity.

The next morning, Joey went downstairs to check-out of the hotel and returned with a beautifully wrapped gift box. My warrior was beaming with delight telling me to sit down and open it right away. I did: it was the stunning outfit I'd admired the night before. Joey, kneeling beside the chair I was sitting in, buried his head in my lap and cried. Not many words were spoken, just the ones that matter; I'm sorry, please forgive me. I accepted his apology and hoped that my heart would soon forget and tear down the protective walls it had been busy building.

We rejoined the band and flew back to LA on July 17, 1975. This time the flight seemed shorter and the water beneath the plane seemed to glisten with promise that everything would be as it was before. I breathed easily as Joey snuggled into my neck and shoulder. I hadn't forgotten what happened in LA but I felt a hell of a lot better.

I flew back to Boston on July 23, 1975. The band would make their way back across the US doing six more shows in just one week. Houston, San Antonio, New Orleans, Tulsa, Kansas City and Dallas would see them before they would come home to the young women who loved them. I ordered an in-flight cocktail to keep from crying. How the hell was I supposed to be mature about this when I was still a broken-hearted child inside? I drank, I slept and silently cried.

I thought of my grandparents in Florida. How the hell did their marriage last fifty years and counting? I wanted to ask them – but I was living in sin as far as they were concerned, not being married to Joey. Their nineteen year-old granddaughter had nowhere to turn for help. I was embarrassed to talk to Terry about it, ashamed to tell my I told-you-so mother and reluctant to share my dirty laundry with the girls at the Club. I longed for a sage wise woman to appear if only to bandage the wound.

I got home to an extremely hot, empty and isolated attic apartment made for midgets. The wall thermometer in our oversized closet of a living room read 112 degrees. It was miserably hot; I had to take two to three showers a day and sit next to a floor fan just to keep from passing out. Joey, still on the road, told me to go out and buy a window air-conditioner for the bedroom. Unfortunately, the windows only opened eleven inches and the smallest air-conditioner I could find was twelve inches high. Joey would be home in a week and he promised that he would find a solution. I might be melted to the floor by then.

Scott Melnick called for Joey. I told him about the scorching heat in our attic apartment and that Joey wouldn't be back until the following week. He offered to come over and help – said he could probably find a solution given that he'd lived in so many old apartments.

Hot, angry and still reeling deep inside my melting heart about Joey's indiscretion, I let the wolf in the door and this time let him kiss me. I knew better but I did it anyway. I felt nothing, revenge sex sucks.

I cleaned up the mess afterwards and sat alone and now self-tainted, in a hot empty apartment. I'd evened the score and I was trying to adopt a new set of rules and amoral conduct. It sucked. I hated myself for having had sex with Scott.

My heart was developing a mind of its own in order to survive. Walls were being constructed with cracked concrete and ivy was taking root. I could see the shadow of doubt on the trails it left behind as it grew in the cracks and crevices of my heart. My rational mind was on a stealth mission to protect me from ever feeling that emotionally injured ever again.

I bought Bonnie Raitt's album with the song, "Sugar Mama," and listened to it over and over again. It became my saving grace mantra in Joey's absence, trying to learn to live without him.

> *"Well I'm sittin' here worryin'*
> *While you're lookin' to find yourself somebody else,*
> *But me lovin' you - nobody but you*
> *You not knowin' what you want yourself*
> *All you pretty, pretty boys used to catch my eye*
> *I just want one who wants to satisfy*
> *Ain't gonna be your sugar mama no more*
> *No, I ain't gonna be your sugar mama no more."*

Bonnie Raitt was a homegrown rebel riding Boston patriot and considerably older than me. I looked to her music for the answers and made her my lyrical mentor. It was me, my echo, my shadow and Bonnie trying to survive the heat of hell and lies of infidelity in one small attic apartment during that record breaking heat wave in Boston. It seemed as if Joey would never get back and when he did, I wouldn't be the same. I'd now joined the ranks of cheaters.

When Joey got home he dropped his bags on the kitchen floor, smiled, closed his eyes and hugged me long and hard, forever it seemed. I kept my eyes deliberately open and looked away, over his shoulder. I remember deciding in that moment, and from then on, that rather than close my eyes and let his love in – all the way into

46

my heart – I would look away. If my eyes were open, I reasoned, part of me would be disconnected so as never to feel that pain again. "It's okay, let him love you more – you've got to save part of yourself in case he strays again. You won't survive unless you do", is what I heard my internal Sugar Mama of a mind dictating to me.

We went into the bedroom and made love. My heart was fine with its newly erected walls but my body remembered the sanctity of our love making. Joey told me that he loved me while tender tears streamed down the sides of my face and onto the pillow behind my head. My heart was his. Who was I trying to kid?

He was home, in our home.

He loved me, and I loved him.

Joey had someone make our bedroom window opening larger and bought a twelve inch air-conditioning unit so at least we'd have one cool room; the room we spent the most time in.

I tried not to count the days before he would be leaving again. He was here now and I would do my best to bring pleasure to every minute of the time we had together. I would make the same boring but tasty meals of broiled scallops, broccoli with hollandaise sauce and a baked potato with butter and sour cream, meatloaf and an occasional baked chicken. I would play soft jazz music and have romantic candles lit on our small kitchen table. I had limited cooking skills at the time but Joey enjoyed everything I made.

Joey's unpacked luggage on the bedroom floor was an unwelcome reminder that in just a few short weeks he would be out on the road touring again. He'd been home for a few days and still had not unpacked his bags, only moved them to the bedroom. He'd taken out his toiletries and the cowboy boots he'd bought for us while in Texas.

While he went new car shopping I began to empty his suitcases to get the laundry ready. When I reached the bottom of the suitcase with all his dirty clothes I slid my hand in the side pocket to make sure I hadn't missed anything. There I found a small folded piece of paper with a girl's name and phone number on it.

My heart stopped before it fell into my chest and fear coursed through my veins again like it had when the girl in LA answered

Joey's phone in his hotel room. No, what is this? Why would he have saved this piece of paper?

Maybe he didn't realize he had it.

Maybe he saved it for someone else.

Maybe it was an innocent business connection or distant relative.

He wouldn't need to offer me any excuses; I was providing them all.

I put it on the night stand and did the laundry. When Joey got back I showed him the large basket of clean, neatly folded laundry. He was pleased that I had taken the initiative to do his laundry. I smiled as I picked up the folded piece of paper off of the night stand that I'd found in his suitcase and asked him if it was something that he needed.

Without looking at me or the piece of paper in my hand he said, "No. That's trash. Throw it out."

I tore it into small pieces and put it in the waste can.

Whatever may have been left over from LA, or any points in-between, was now gone.

Joey asked me to come outside and see what he'd bought. It was a brand spanking new red Corvette with gray smoked T-tops and beige leather interior. He had traded in his beloved LT-1 Corvette and this is what we'd be taking to Joe and Elyssa's wedding the next day.

On August 5, Joe Perry, lead guitarist for the band and longtime girlfriend, Elyssa Jarret, were married at the Ritz Carlton in Boston. This was the beginning of lush, extravagant and wasted Aerosmith laps of indecent luxury.

Here's what I remember about Joe and Elyssa's wedding at the Ritz. I remember pulling up to valet park the car at the elaborate entrance to the hotel and within seconds having my door opened by an ornately uniformed doorman. I waited for Joey to walk around the car and join me. We walked into the hotel holding hands and were told that the "event" was upstairs. Rock and roll clad, long haired (some scary looking) people were everywhere.

We were warmly greeted by Elyssa who was wearing a champagne colored tea length chiffon dress and a smile that could have lit the entire room. By her side was her lovely, socially graced mother making introductions and also welcoming guests. Joe, usually inseparable from Elyssa, was nowhere to be seen.

White gloved waiters walked throughout the crystal chandeliered ballroom serving guests extravagantly prepared and beautifully presented food on silver trays while another group of smiling servers freely poured the best bubbly.

I was uncomfortable not knowing anyone but the band and its entourage; Joey held my hand tightly with the promise of not letting go.

Guests without an appetite for food were buzzing around asking where the bathrooms were. Many were asking where Joe was. Some were talking about Steven having worn feathers to the wedding in a deliberate attempt to upstage the bride. Most people accused Steven of being impulsive, impetulant and impervious to what anyone thought while others agreed he was just being Steven – clever, cute and flamboyant. I weighed in on the side of him being cute, adorable in fact, in a custom made feathered suit.

Everything seemed so awkward, except for Elyssa. This was her wedding day and she made one beautiful bride.

Soon it was over and the same flock of rockers made their way out of the Ritz Carlton in much the same fashion as they'd entered; irreverently unique, confidently united and high to the gills.

Joey and I stopped on the way home to buy a bottle of Dom Perignon champagne and a gram of coke to enjoy in our cool little nest. We both knew the time was quickly approaching when Joey would be headed back out on the road and we were determined to love and connect as best we could in the time remaining.

Joey was concerned about leaving me alone for so much of the time while he was touring. On a Wednesday morning in late August, Joey offered to drive me to work and pick me up, telling me that he wanted to spend every moment possible together. I finished my lunch shift at the Club and walked out to the car where Joey was waiting on the Playboy parking lot. When I opened the door he said, "I have a surprise for you." He reached behind the seats and gently pulled out a small blanket with something moving inside. He pulled the blanket down and there was the cutest Yorkshire terrier pup face I'd ever seen. Joey said, "I don't want you to miss me too much, Nan, and I want you to have company while I'm gone."

I reached for the small cuddly pup and felt my heart quiver. I held him close and sprinkled tears all over him. Joey said he was the real deal and he had the breeding papers for him but I'd have to name him. I named him Nathaniel Whitney Kramer and called him Nathan. Nate would be his nickname.

Joey left a few days later for shows in Cleveland, Trenton, Richmond, Largo, Maryland and New York. On August 27, Nathan and I flew into DC to join him for the Maryland and New York shows. Nate was about to have a very early introduction to living on the road and staying in hotels. For $15 most airlines would let him fly under my seat in a kennel. Every hotel had at least two glass ashtrays in the room which served as food and water bowls.

On August 29, 1975 the band played at Shaeffer Music center in NY and we stayed at the Warwick Hotel. It was a big deal. The band's third album, "Toys" had just gone gold and Leber-Krebs was planning a special reception for us at the home of Steve Leber on Long Island. They sent separate limos for each of the band members – so we really felt important hogging up the whole back of one car. Nathan flew better than he rode in cars; he threw up on the back seat of the limo on the long ride out to the Leber's home. I felt terrible but Joey assured me that the backseat of limousines had seen far worse than this before.

When we arrived at the Lebers' home, Steve Leber, his wife and David Krebs were waiting outside to greet us. I sensed that this was a real shebang; I could smell money lavishly spent everywhere. It was catered, Aladdin style decorated; whatever you want, your wish is my command. We ate, we drank and accepted presents. Each band member was presented with a framed gold record for "Toys" and all of us, band members and their significant others were given a solid gold, custom made, numbered on the back, Aerosmith wing shaped necklace. Fourteen necklaces were made in all, ten for us and four more for the Krebs and the Lebers. Mine had the lucky number thirteen on the back. I remember thinking how indecent it all seemed, and yet we allowed ourselves to be consciously seduced.

After our stay at the Warwick Hotel in New York in late August of 1975, it was back to work in Boston for me and out on the road for Joey and the band. On one of our nightly calls from the road, Joey asked if I would visit Julia, Steven's girlfriend. He said Steven was concerned about her spending too much time alone and would I please go over to their apartment and just keep her company.

I remember going to visit her only once while they were away. She answered the door looking like an astronaut wearing a silver foiled, one-piece jumpsuit that covered all but her neck, hands and feet. She said she had a severe skin condition and a doctor prescribed a special cream to be worn under the odd looking suit. I found her to be very sweet, childlike and totally in love with Steven. Julia was only sixteen but seemed like a child born to an earlier time; like the 1920's or 30's. She talked to me about Cole Porter's music, life and lyrics and "scatting." Julia explained that "scatting" is a way of singing without real words and rhymically demonstrated a few lovely bars. She said that Steven was so good at it and she hoped that someday he would do it on an album or at a live performance. What impressed me the most was how sweet tempered she was and that she drank three glasses of milk during our two-hour visit.

Shortly after our visit, their apartment caught fire and Julia had to be hospitalized for smoke inhalation, or so I was told. There were rumors that she'd deliberately set the fire to get Steven home. I didn't believe that for a second. It was only a few years ago that I learned that she was pregnant and forced to have a late term abortion while in the hospital.

You would think that if your house burns down, you'd get a little time off, right? Time to find a new home, replace your belongings, make sure your loved ones are okay. No, this did not hold true in the highly financed world of rock and roll in the seventies. In fact, the boys were back out on the road so quickly after the fire in Steven's apartment that much of the burden to replace everything was left up to a few people who worked for the band and stayed behind.

Steven asked me if I would take my small TV that wasn't being used over to the new place so that Julia would have something to watch. Someone needed to watch over her. Joey told me it wasn't my problem and they'd get it worked out, just get the TV over there.

Ray Tabano helped Julia a lot I'm sure, and Steven's clothes designer, Francine Larnis, was a good friend to Julia. Ray was also busy getting the new recording space, The Aerosmith Wherehouse, set up in Waltham so the guys could do pre-production recording at home in Boston rather than in New York.

The Wherehouse opened with a big Halloween Bash and I got back from Miami just in time to find a costume to wear. Joey had forgotten my twentieth birthday the week before and with so much going on with the band; I didn't remind him of it. Instead, I flew to Miami to visit my grandparents for a few days. He went to New York. We weren't communicating well and the band was consuming everyone's attention. When Joey called me in Miami I told him about my forgotten birthday and he asked me to meet him in New York and we'd drive back to Boston together.

Thank God romance was alive again. Joey was there to meet my plane and could hardly wait to get me back to the car, filled with birthday presents. Lush, lovely, especially hand picked thoughtful and romantic presents, beautifully wrapped were waiting to be opened. There was a French rabbit fur coat, the softest thing I've ever felt, silk camisoles, pretty panties, perfume and a solid gold heart necklace with a diamond star in the center. Oh, I was a happy girl and the lovemaking in the car wasn't too shabby either, even with a stick shift.

Knowing how much I wanted to get back to school and pay for it myself, Joey encouraged me to sell my car and save the money to put toward tuition. He said he wanted to buy a family car for us that would be mostly mine, but available to him when the weather was bad and he couldn't drive the new red Corvette. He bought the ugliest, puke green, standard shift, four-speed Chevy Monza I'd ever seen. Its only saving grace was that it was new and had air conditioning. After being pulled over a few times in the red Corvette for speeding, Joey sold it to a nice couple and bought a white Corvette with chocolate brown leather interior. It was a beauty, a very sexy Playboy beauty and an automatic.

About a month before Christmas, 1975, Joey was away and my sweet six month old puppy and I were safely tucked under the covers late on a Saturday night, watching television. I had just smoked a little pot hoping that it might divert my attention away from missing Joey.

We had the only dog in the old house with four apartments; the other tenants had cats. I'd noticed earlier that day that Nathan had stuffed one of Joey's long sleeved cotton shirts into a hole just above the baseboard in our bedroom. I thought it a bit odd, but assumed that when the workers renovated the attic apartment before we moved in, they must have forgotten to patch or fill this three inch hole. I remember admiring the skill I imagined that my little pup must have had to shove Joey's shirt so tightly into the hole and how pleased Joey would be with Nate's intelligence. I would tell him the next time he called home.

I was starting to drift off to sleep when I heard rapidly descending chalkboard like scratching sounds coming down the wall above the shirt stuffed hole and then a running sound on the carpet. Nathan leaped off the bed and ran to the corner of the room where my vanity table sat. The only light in the room was coming from the television at the foot of the bed. I couldn't see beyond the TV but I heard horrific animal rumbling and high pitched squealing. I didn't know what Nate was tangling with but I was very much aware of his four pound size and instinctively knew that he was unfairly matched. Without thinking, I drew out the strongest commanding voice that I could muster and called him back to the bed. Thankfully, he heeded my command and returned to the bed with half of his tender pink and black nose bloody and missing. I grabbed him and hung on for dear life.

The kitchen night light just outside the bedroom was on and I saw not one, but two, fully grown bigger than cats, wharf rats run across the bedroom floor and into the kitchen. Shaking now, frozen in fear, I held Nathan tightly and told him," No." I grabbed a tissue from the bedside table, gently wiped the blood from his nose and was pissed that half of it was gone.

It was now 3:00 a.m. Who the hell do you call in the middle of the night when your home has been invaded by giant rats and the only way out happens to be in the same direction that they ran? It sounded like they were having a feast in the kitchen and I was scared to death to move from the bed. The itinerary for where the band was staying was in another room so I couldn't call Joey. I called Terry and she called Ray Tabano. Ray called me, assessed the situation, assured me that the beastly intruders would be gone by daylight, and that he'd be over at dawn to get Nathan and me out of the apartment. He said I should pack a few things and he'd take me to a hotel.

No way. I wasn't moving off my bed; he could rescue me in my pajamas and take me to a hotel with the clothes on my back. It seemed like forever until the sun came up, but it did, and Raymond took Nathan and me a few miles down the road to a Holiday Inn. He managed to reach Joey and told him what happened and where to reach me.

Joey was furious when he called me, I think mostly because he couldn't come home to take care of the situation himself. He told me he'd be back in a week; I should get out of the hotel, stay with Terry and find us another place to live – closer to the rest of the band, in Brookline. And, he said I should call the landlord and tell him why we were breaking the lease and leaving.

Our landlord was dismissive; he said that maybe I'd seen a mouse or a squirrel but definitely not a rat. He said he would set traps up anyway and that I should return to the apartment as he would not allow us to break the lease.

I hadn't found a new apartment yet but I needed to get back into the old one to get clothes and cosmetics; I was still working at Playboy. One morning before work I called the landlord to ask if he'd checked the traps because I needed to get in. He assured me that he had and tried once more to placate me. I didn't trust him. I went to the apartment and found boxed food strewn everywhere and two small aluminum pans of poison pellets sitting undisturbed on the kitchen floor. I grabbed my cosmetics, a few clothes and quickly got the hell out of there. Why in the hell would rats eat poison when they had the run of the open-shelved pantry?

I called the landlord again, threatened to call the health department and he said he would go ahead and set glue traps even though he was certain it was unnecessary. What a prick.

I'd forgotten to grab my curlers and hairdryer so the next day I called again, "Have you checked the traps? I'm on my way over to the apartment."

"Yes, Miss Karlson. There are no rats in your apartment."

I sensed an imminent showdown with a two-legged rat and something had me grab the Polaroid camera to take with me. As I entered the apartment I saw the glue trap; it was the size of a boot box lid. In it sat a squealing, wide mouthed rat whose body filled the 11x14 trap and his tail extended about twelve inches beyond that. He was mighty and flailing his glue trapped stuck body with great force across the kitchen floor. Shaking, I took a Polaroid shot and went downstairs to borrow a neighbor's phone and called the landlord. He sent his brother over with a baseball bat to kill the sucker once and for all. The hideously disgusting rat murderous act took him twenty minutes. I grabbed my hair tools and left the bastard there with the dead rat at his feet. He and his wiseass brother could figure it out: Joey and I needed a new home.

I found a gorgeous two bedroom, ground floor apartment on James Street in Coolidge Corner. It was humongous, with ten rooms and a screened in back porch. French doors, wood floors, built in pantry and a breakfast nook, living room, den and formal dining room – lovely and affordable. Mr. Chin, our new landlord, assured me that we would make many happy memories there. When Joey got home he went over to Waban Street with his pellet gun and shot the whole place to smithereens.

The first happy memory we made at 19 James Street was in the Master Bedroom shower. It was an oversized 5' x 6' 1940's designed steam spa shower that housed eight spigots, top to bottom. The water pressure wasn't great but we were delighted just the same with the playful spray of strategically placed water faucets.

Body waxing was considered to be barbaric at the time so I would shave my lovely garden for work as a Playboy Bunny. Joey had the inspired idea after our first James Street shower for me to let him shave me for my Playboy costume. The bathroom was filled with warm steam from the long shower we'd just enjoyed. He asked me to sit on the toilet as he warmed the shaving cream. Opening my robe, he instructed me to lay back and let him do his magic on my mound. I complied, and he took his time to meticulously sculpt a beautiful shape, front to back with his razor. I remember the expression on his face was as intensely focused as that of a great master artist and he was well pleased with his work. Joey approached everything he did with serious, flawless dedication.

Most of his stage clothes had to be hand-washed and gently hung on a rack above the tub to dry. On my first attempt to wash his Danskin stage-wear, I hung them up to dry, crooked on the rod. Joey told me he appreciated the effort, but if I was going to do something, do it right. Hang them straightly, right-side up and far enough apart to ensure even drying, is what he told me. Thank you, Mrs. Doris Kramer, for teaching him so well. I've never forgotten that lesson and to this day have a do-it-right or don't-do-it-at-all approach to everything I undertake.

My mom was so worried about me. I was barely twenty years old, had epilepsy, a job as a Playboy Bunny, a musician for a boyfriend, and had just survived a wharf rat attack. She asked Joey and me to please come to Baltimore, even if just for one night. We did and she made us an unforgettable meal. It was there the idea of re-releasing "Dream On" as a single record was hatched.

Joey took the golden egg and ran with it, all the way to money maker David Krebs. David was smart, sexy and not that much older than the bands he represented. He flew all the way to the record company and convinced them that he had the fortuitous golden egg for Aerosmith. The rest is Aerosmith history.

Three Peas in a Pod,
Patty, Me and Jill

Joey and the Mona Lisa
Smile

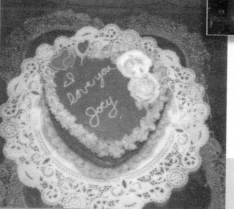

True Confession

Where It All Began

Mickey and
Doris Kramer

Me and My Lucille
Ball Eyebrows

Annabelle, Suzy and Amy

58

Sexy New Bangs
(first in-salon haircut)
19 James Street, Brookline, MA

Nathaniel Whitney
Kramer and Joey—
"I don't want you
to miss me too
much Nan".

The Ladies White Corvette!

Jeff Beck Curious
About Joey's Bunny

Me Easing Joey's Fears

Rock Scene Coverage of Show
at Comiskey Park 1976

Rock Scene Magazine
November, 1975
Playboy Club Detroit

Got My Eye On You—
Tom Hamilton

Terry and I Tripping in NYC
(1970's low-tech selfie)
St. Regis Hotel

Saturday Night Live
at the Hamilton's

Our Chanukah Bush

Is This Boat Big Enough?

Joey and His New NIKON

Terry and I Tanning Our
Silly White Asses

PROFESSIONAL & COY LIP LOCK—STEVEN TYLER & SUSIE Q

Track **5**

FIVE RING CIRCUS – Where's the Ring?

"I took my love and I took it down
I climbed a mountain and I turned around
And I saw my reflection in the snow-covered hills
Till the landslide brought me down
Oh, mirror in the sky, what is love?
Can the child within my heart rise above?
Can I sail through the changing ocean tides?
Can I handle the seasons of my life?
Well, I've been afraid of changing
'Cause I've built my life around you
But time makes you bolder
Even children get older
And I'm getting older too"
-- Fleetwood Mac

Terry fell in love with Fleetwood Mac and married Tom Hamilton. Joey bought the new Fleetwood Mac album with the song, "Landslide." The earth was shaking and the world, as we'd known it, was spinning out of control.

A landslide, a windfall of money, was coming in from the first three albums going gold and eventually platinum, following the re-release of "Dream On." Our lives quickly became an indecent, insane and an indescribable merry-go-round in 1976. "Dream On" was climbing the charts with a bullet, depositing more money into the already doomsday driven dollar making machine of Aerosmith and I wanted to get off the ride because I could barely hold on.

It was far worse for the guys because they were the ones in the spotlight being bathed in money and showered with adulation. It got to the point where we could no longer go out in public in Boston without being hounded by fans. I hated it. Joey could usually slip past the fans without being recognized, but Tom, tall, lanky and naturally blessed with platinum blonde hair that made the moon pale, forget it. We ate in a lot, mostly at Tom and Terry's apartment.

Saturday nights were the best of times with Tom and Terry. We'd eat late, drink a little wine, smoke a little pot and then watch Saturday Night Live with the original cast of wet your pants players. We'd laugh our asses off with what they were able to get away with on the show. Best of times and many treasured memories we had with Tom and Terry. Like Ricky and Lucy with Fred and Ethel, they were our best friends and we made an awesome foursome; two Jews (Joey and Terry) and two Goyim (me and Tom).

After the rats on Waban Street and before the boys came home from touring, Terry and I put up a real Christmas tree in her apartment and called it a Chanukah Bush. We made a big ten inch, three-dimensional Star of David out of red construction and paper and glued sexy pictures from Playboy Magazine on the three sides of the star. We hung gaudy decorations all over it and tossed silver foiled tinsel from top to bottom. The boys were pleased with our efforts when they saw what we'd created and we enjoyed a quiet little Christmas together, before heading off to see our other families.

I had to work at the Club on New Year's Eve so Joey dressed up in a suit and tie and came in to see me and made sure he was there at midnight to steal a kiss from me. It was a lot of fun waiting on him, dressed in that sexy Playboy costume. He handed me a new hundred dollar bill before he left and told me he'd see me at home. He had a bottle of chilled Dom Perignon and a little tray of food waiting in the living room for us to enjoy. It was an anniversary of sorts – it had been a year since the first time he told me he loved me, when I pretended not to hear him.

In February of 1976, the four of us traveled together to Miami for Brad and Lori's wedding. We went straight from the Miami Airport to the beach I grew up on at 71st and Collins. Who cared that it was almost midnight? Terry and I ran through the sand fully clothed and jumped in the ocean. The guys laughed hysterically. Terry's watch was waterproof, but sadly, mine was not.

We were dripping wet when we entered the hotel lobby to check-in. The hotel had screwed up our reservations and said they only had one room for us, one room with two single beds. Joey had a new Nikon camera and we set the thing on auto-shoot to snap pictures of ourselves while we jumped on the beds and pretended to be homosexual, wife swapping pranksters.

Lori's parents put a plywood dance floor over their swimming pool for the private wedding. The song "Feelings," played as they took their first dance as man and wife. Everyone looked for the bathrooms to snort coke while drinking champagne. Most people followed Steven around, knowing he'd be the first to cop Miami blow. He was. He did. On a boat in Bal Harbor, he copped enough to share and give a nice wedding present to the newly wed couple.

Tom, Terry, Joey and I moved to the Newport Hotel on 163rd Street. The boys went deep sea fishing while Terry and I baked in the sun. Our skinny white asses were pale from a long-ass Boston winter.

My mom was scheduled to have surgery the first week in March and her television, an old black and white one, had just died. Joey bought her a new color Sony TV from Lechmere's in Boston and arranged to have me take it on the plane to Baltimore, with his best wishes and a huge thank you for "Dream On." I flew to Baltimore on March 3 and stayed for a week to help Mom after her surgery. She was well pleased with the Sony and Joey's generosity.

On March 10th, I joined Joey and the band in New York as they were finishing up the work on "Rocks." This would be their fourth album and everyone was crazy, thinking that it might ship platinum following the success of sky rocketing sales. "Dream On" had made it to number 6 on the Billboard charts.

Leber-Krebs put us up in the St. Regis Hotel. The nail biting psychotic film, "Taxi," had just been released and we were able to watch it in our hotel room. A demented Robert DeNiro scared the crap out of our happy foursome when he pulled his yellow cab up to the curb at the St. Regis Hotel in the movie!

The boys went to the Record Plant (studio) to work on the album with Jack Douglas and Jay Messina while Terry showed me how to shop in New York. We started at Bloomingdale's in the lingerie department. Next we hit the fragrance counter where I fell in love with and purchased a small brown vile of Tea Rose essential oil. I couldn't get enough of it and it became my signature fragrance.

Coming down the escalator in Bloomie's we spotted Gilda Radner, from Saturday Night Live, going up. She was our heroine and we had to follow her. We ran down the remaining escalator stairs and hopped on the escalator going up; we had to catch up to her and say hello. When we caught up to the back of her long curly reddish locks, we were scared silly and afraid to speak to her. We let her pass and went back to the hotel.

Terry had brought some LSD with her to New York. The boys would be working for most of the night, if not through the night, so we dropped acid. I'd only tried it once before as a teenager in Miami Beach the night before Easter and it was an eye-opening experience. I trusted Terry and I couldn't think of a better person to do it with again. We were laughing so hard at nothing and hanging our heads out of the tenth story window in her hotel room, in the pouring down rain, when the chain broke on the heart necklace that Joey had given me for my birthday. I managed to grab the chain but not before the solid gold heart fell ten stories in slow motion down to the wide sidewalk on a busy New York street.

Terry, usually taking the lead in everything we did together said,

"Oh nooooooo, we'll never find it!"

I saw exactly where my heart landed, twelve inches from the curb with deep rain water rivering down the street alongside of it.

"Come on, yes we will!" I determinedly declared.

Terry grabbed the room key and we made a beeline for the elevator. It came quickly and we ran outside to the street. I grabbed my heart off the pavement and we both shouted up at the sky and did a little gratitude rain dance on the street in front of the St. Regis Hotel.

"Rocks" shipped platinum in early May and Terry and I flew to Detroit to meet up with our guys on May 7th. On May 9th, we all flew to New York for a really big show at Madison Square Garden.

Joey's mom, lover that she was and proponent for us tying the marriage knot soon, bought Joey and me matching black velvet jumpsuits to wear to the concert. I ran all over Manhattan for hours trying to find the right shoes. Every shoe I liked had more than a two-inch heel and I couldn't make myself be taller than Joey, not at the Garden. How awkward would that be? I wanted my man to tower above me and shine in his own light. I didn't want to be the taller than he Bunny beside him. I was always careful about the shoes I wore around Joey.

The band's performance was grand and after the show, Joey and I, in our matching black velvet jumpsuits, greeted his mom, sisters, John Belushi, from the cast of Saturday Night Live, and Linda Blair from the 1973 supernatural horror film, "The Exorcist." Linda, the possessed child actress in the movie, had just turned seventeen and had a huge crush on Steven. Julia Holcomb, Steven's girlfriend, was eighteen and no match for the charms of this big screen she-devil vixen. The guys and Kelly managed to reel Steven back in before things got out of hand with the underage baby faced star. Julia really had nothing to worry about; she was a year older than Linda, a more experienced and prettier temptress and happened to be holding Steven's cocaine stash. Her man wouldn't leave her high and dry; she had the goods.

The guys had ten more shows to do in May and about five thousand miles to cover in sixteen days. Before joining them on May 22, in Atlanta, Terry and I took a little side trip of our own to Cape Cod with Ray Tabano and my old boyfriend from Baltimore, Andy Bialczak. I don't remember which car Terry and Raymond drove, but Andy and

I took Joey's pretty white Corvette. Andy had owned a vintage red Corvette when we were in high school and was chafing at the bit to get behind Joey's new car and open it up. It was an innocent, fun time and Raymond and Andy made sure that no trouble found us.

Much to Joey's dismay, Andy and I drove the Corvette to Baltimore. I assured Joey that Andy was an experienced and safe driver. Andy was also in the process of getting his pilot's license which is what brought him to Boston in the first place. Still, Joey wasn't happy about it and that put a lot of pressure on me.

Since my ticket was issued roundtrip Baltimore to Atlanta, I had Mom drive me to the airport in Joey's car. We were late and I was rushing. The chain on my heart necklace broke again and fell down the bathroom sink drain at my mother's house. I'd had to wait for a plumber to come and retrieve it. Mom drove fast but not fast enough for me to catch my plane. The ticket agent refused to let me board and we argued for five minutes before the plane took off. I had to get to Atlanta, Joey was already unhappy with me. The stress of the situation and the unsympathetic ticket agent made my blood boil and my brain short circuit and - shut down – seizure time – right there in the airport.

Thank God Mom had parked the car and come in to the airport to make sure I'd made the flight. I was crying hysterically by the time I regained consciousness. Here's the blessing and the curse of grand mal seizures; you don't remember anything that happened. Always, after a grand mal seizure – the one that makes you shake, convulse, eyes roll back in your head and fall to the ground losing consciousness – you don't remember the experience. That's the gift. You are, however, pissed off, blurting out angry unformed words at self-concerned gawkers and spectators as you try to regain your memory of what the hell just happened. You're disoriented and disbelieving as a few smart ones in the crowd try to explain to you that you've just had a seizure. It's the worst feeling in the world to lose control of your faculties in this way.

After ten or fifteen minutes you've drawn an unwelcome crowd of curious onlookers who whisper amongst themselves how tragic this is. You can see the revealing fear in their faces that says they hope and pray this never happens to them. And they don't leave. They want to know what happens next.

Disgusted, with limbs that feel like they should be on tree trunks rather than attached to your torso, you do your best to stand up. Usually one kind, compassionate person will help you get to your feet. The whispering crowd dies down but still watches on and you just want to tell them all to fuck off.

Memory slowly returns and you are blessed to never have brain recall of the convulsions; the absolute loss of control over your physical body. Not everyone pees their pants as commonly thought – I don't. It's really hard to swallow your tongue, so forget putting anything in a convulsing person's mouth; you could lose a finger and they could incur a costly teeth-breaking dental bill.

It's fine to move furniture and rest something soft under the person's head if it's banging on a hard floor. Otherwise, don't try to restrain their involuntary movements, it will be over soon. Let it happen and do your best to remain calm. Let them be and if it's me, don't call an ambulance. It's over in ten minutes.

Epilepsy simply means seizure; it can happen to anyone at anytime. I believe that new cases can be due to head injuries, tumors, strokes, infections, but often the causes can't be found. Drinking too much alcohol can bring on a seizure or a high fever with children. Mine came with the onset of a head injury, birth control pills to regulate my periods, and the stress of divorcing parents. I also had a propensity for a seizure disorder having an aunt with severe, uncontrollable epileptic fits, as they were called in her day.

Most people are fortunate in that their seizures can be successfully controlled with medication. Some, like me, have an "aura" or warning prior to the onset of a grand mal seizure. For me, it presents as stuttering and an involuntary upward jerking of my arms, as if I were a marionette and someone suddenly yanked the strings up.

I know when this "aura" appears it's time to stop whatever I'm doing and seek the shelter of a soft bed and take more anticonvulsant medication as I try to sleep. It will usually pass quickly and is always a sign for me that I need to pay attention to my well-being.

Lack of sleep and stress are the two biggest triggers for me and with knowing how angry Joey was that Andy and I drove the Vet from Boston to Baltimore without asking him, I was highly stressed, un-nerved and anxious to get to Atlanta. Dropping my gold heart necklace down the drain and having to wait for a plumber didn't help either. Mom having trepidation about driving Joey's sports car and the hold-the-line, make no exceptions, gate keeper agent...it all added up to make one perfect storm of a grand mal seizure at the Baltimore airport. I'm sure it was quite a show.

Mom got me back to her place and I tried to reach Joey to let him know I'd missed the plane. He didn't answer the phone in his room. At that time the band used the name, "The Shakespearean Players" when they traveled so that fans couldn't find them at their hotels. Steven registered as Laurence Olivier and Joey as George Bernard Shaw. Neither one of them answered their phones that night. I couldn't remember anyone else's alias. Jeff Beck, on the same tour with Aerosmith, was registered as "Jeff Beck." I called the hotel again and asked for his room. I told him who I was and asked him to please tell Joey that everything was okay, but I'd missed my plane and I'd fly out the following day.

I got a good night's sleep and Mom drove me to the airport again, arriving an hour before take-off. In those days, before 9/11, there was no TSA or long security lines to go though, and you could almost always get on the flight even if they had shut the plane's door. You could smoke on planes too.

Joey wasn't happy with me when I finally reached Atlanta but decided to forgive me just the same when he saw that Jeff Beck was curious about his young Bunny.

The airport seizure had taxed me terribly, and I wasn't bouncing back as quickly as I had done previously after a seizure. I was losing weight from the stress of travel, work and the crazy whirlwind our lives had become. There was no time for anything and I often forgot to eat or just didn't want to be bothered with what it took to cook for one in Joey's absence.

The good news was that I no longer fit into my tangerine Playboy Bunny costume and Suki had moved on leaving her canary yellow and bright turquoise suits behind. They fit my 110 pound frame perfectly.

My mom was worried sick about what was happening to me. She called my neurologist in Baltimore who convinced her that I should agree to go to Johns Hopkins hospital for a week of evaluation. The doctor told my mom that something else, like a brain tumor or lesion in the brain, could be causing the breakthrough with seizures. The term "breakthrough" in epilepsy refers to seizures reoccurring. They now had my attention.

I tried to make light of it with Joey; he had enough to deal with inside the business of the band. The drug use and feuding between Steven Tyler and Joe Perry had gotten way out of hand. They wrote ninety percent of the songs so they had more money to piss away on heroin – a very expensive drug at the time. Joey didn't need one more thing to worry about.

Joey wrote me a letter while I was at Hopkins and gave it to me when I got back to Boston. We'd only been in the apartment for five minutes when he insisted that I sit down and read it. I'd never seen a happier man watching a woman reading a letter in my life. Joey was deliriously happy and grateful to God that nothing was wrong with me other than having a neurological disorder called epilepsy.

I wanted to read it again. This time, I let all the words into my heart as we sat in our brown velvet playpen of a couch. I cried over each page and he just kept grinning, ear to ear grinning, decidedly proud of himself. He sat so close to me in his worn dark corduroy pants with his thighs resting perfectly next to mine that I could feel his muscles as they trembled beside me. I finished reading the letter for the second time and we made mind blowing love right there on the couch below the bay front window.

On June 9th, 1976, Joey and I flew to New York to buy his dad a Cadillac for Father's Day. Joey originally wanted to buy him a

Mercedes but didn't think his dad would be appreciative of German engineering in any form. We took a cab from the airport to the car dealership and picked out a gorgeous cherry red hummer of a car, ostentatiously manufactured in the USA.

Joey was so excited to blow his father's mind with a new car. He was certainly more excited about the outlandish gift than his dad. Mickey was mad. Why did his son spend all his money on a ridiculous red car? He kept the car but Joey was scarred with deep wounds, the depth of which I hadn't realized until that day.

Joey's mom liked the car and the attention it gathered from neighbors in the driveway. She was proud that yes, her son, could afford to buy his dad a present such as this. She also had a gift for me. Knowing how concerned Joey had been about my seizure disorder and time in the hospital, she gave me a small, round antiqued silver and mother of pearl pillbox that I could carry with me so that I'd always have Dilantin on hand. Sweet, sweet gesture and I deeply appreciated the love and thoughtfulness with which it was given.

June 12th, we traveled to Pontiac, Michigan and Joey did his first drum solo. The band was back on the road fiercely grinding it out night after night. They did twelve shows all across the US in seventeen days.

Back in Boston, Terry and I went to the Bicentennial Fourth of July Fireworks celebration on the Charles River. I parked the pretty white Lady's Vet just off Storrow Drive and we sat on top of it to watch the amazing display of Boston proud fireworks. It was a natural high distraction from missing our guys and soon we'd be joining them again on the road.

On July 9th, we flew to Chicago for the sold out concert at Comiskey Park, an outdoor baseball field and the home of the Chicago White Sox. A very stupid fan lit a small cherry bomb in the bleachers and the park caught fire. We were rushed to nearby band trailers and waited it out while the firemen secured the grounds. It was the perfect opportunity for the press to obtain a few interviews while everyone had to remain still in one place.

Joey and I went to the trailer of Rick Derringer and his wife, Liz. I enjoyed getting to know an older Derringer, who at seventeen had a band called the McCoy's that recorded the iconic song, *"Hang on Sloopy"* in 1965. Liz was extremely nice and hospitable.

I left Joey on the road to get back to work in Boston and register for the fall semester. It wasn't Boston College, as I'd once impossibly hoped for; I was registering for full-time classes and a two-year degree in Interior Design at Chamberlain Junior College. Joey thought that would be my best pursuit given that we would be building, designing, and decorating a cabin in the woods of New Hampshire. He wanted me to be hands on with creating our new permanent residence.

I didn't know what I wanted to study; I'd always enjoyed writing and speaking Spanish but didn't have a clue what to do with those two passions. I gave up the idea of becoming a translator at the United Nations in New York. I still loved writing, keeping journals, and I wrote poetry and short stories that no one would ever read. I lacked the confidence to become a writer because I'd failed English in my senior year of high school and then failed to pass the required Review English at the community college in Baltimore. No, writing just wasn't in the cards for me.

Other than playing a major role in creating our haven in the woods, I don't know what Joey thought I'd ever do with a degree in Interior Design. New Hampshire wasn't well populated at that time. I registered and used my own money from the sale of my car to pay for it just the same.

Early August would bring the band back to Boston for regional performances. Late August would take them back to Hawaii. I would be starting school in September.

I wish I'd never tried to help Joey unpack from road trips. Before they left for Hawaii – he said it would cost too much to take me this time and after all, I'd be starting school – I did his damn unpacking for laundry again. He was busy working out and deciding which first Rolex watch he should buy. Two pieces of paper this time tucked in his luggage, both with girls' names and numbers. I didn't want to bring it up again and I didn't want to know. I had my treasure chest of a letter, and he loved me. I'd heard about the ten day rule for guys on the road and it was a battle I didn't think I could win.

The band went to Hawaii and I went to Miami, pissed. I set out to even the infidelity score even though Bonnie Raitt sang,

"You can't have love, people, when you're keepin' score."

I loved Joey, he loved me and we both cheated, it's as simple as that. I'd have to learn to do it as well as he did it and maybe even learn to like it. I'll give you a little hint; I never did learn to like it.

I disappeared in Miami for four days while Joey and my family tried unsuccessfully to reach me. I was strongly pursued by a wealthy, good looking young man, a year older than me. I called the escapade nursing my wounds and preparing for the semester. I made up a story to give Joey about where I'd been. He was in Hawaii without me and when he came back he'd be getting ready to leave for the band's first European tour. I'd be in school and as Joey pointed out again, it was not economically feasible for him to take me with him. Bullshit.

And I hated these unspoken agreements and rules of the road:

- Sex on the road is okay; it doesn't mean anything.

- Be loyal to your band mates and don't tell on them.

- Wear a condom and try to do it someplace other than your own hotel room, unless there are two of them and they're both really special.

- Lastly, the ten day rule. Only blow jobs for the ten days prior to going home.

Bullshit. You play or you stray. They'll grow up one day and never be out on that long and winding, wandering to hell road again, I naively thought.

Paris: I hated to miss Paris, and England, and Scotland, and Germany, and Sweden and Holland, and Switzerland. I'd be sitting in classrooms studying architecture and interior design and spending my 21st birthday alone while the band was on tour.

Bonnie Raitt didn't help; neither did Fleetwood Mac, Bob Marley or the drummer in the house band at the Playboy Club who could sing. Gene Perkins, general manager of the Club helped a little. More than twice my age, handsome, smart and funny, he was in search of a new Bunny and wanted to introduce me to the delicacy of freshly caught lobster off the coast of Maine and other assorted New England tea party pleasures. I'd be lying if I said it was mainly lobster.

I'm not proud of my escapades but they were how I learned to survive Joey's.

Joey's parents had a young friend from their neighborhood that was also a drummer and really looked up to Joey. The barely starting to shave high school student was having a hard time at home with his parents. Mickey and Doris thought it would be good for him to get away for a few days and perhaps might even be of help to me while Joey was away. We agreed that he could visit.

Scott Sobol was barely seventeen when he came to visit us in Boston. I wanted to be a positive role model for him; I went outside to smoke when I needed a break from the intricate drafting homework I'd been working on. It was a Sunday, as I remember, and I was sitting in the den where I'd set up my drafting table and all the tools I needed to finish the project due on Monday.

I'd worked hard on the design, a new type of highly functional classroom for children in daycare and I'd given tremendous thought to each and every detail. Even though my hands were unexplainably and uncontrollably flying upwards above my drafting table as I tried to steady the mechanical pencil in my hand, I was determined to finish it and turn it in on time.

This was the first time I'd ever felt like a marionette with strings attached to my body, with a force outside of myself, yanking the strings up from above.

Suddenly, my hands flew up one last time and both feet jerked forward breaking the frame of the table before it and I went crashing to the floor.

When I regained consciousness, I was in an ambulance, confused, pissed off and had a bloody hand. Evidently, when the mechanical pencil flew out of my hand during the seizure, it returned to earth and found a target in the back of my right hand.

A very worried young man, whom I almost recognized as Scott Sobol, was trying to reassure me in the ambulance. It must have scared the hell out of him when he heard the crash and saw me seizing on the floor.

I was admitted to the hospital and they called my mom. I assured her that I would be fine and that maybe my medication was low. As it turns out, it wasn't the level of anticonvulsants in my blood; it was the damn intense eye-hand coordination that set the seizure off. To this day, I can't tie a bow or wrap a package without triggering seizure activity in my brain and the reminder of the event remains in a dark lead pencil mark on the top of my right hand.

When I returned to school on Wednesday to turn in my project late, I was also late for class. The instructor was taking roll call as I walked in the door. He stopped calling names and turned to look at me as I was entering the classroom. With the meanest and most sarcastic voice I'd ever heard he said,

"And what is your saga today, Miss Karlson?"

Humiliated, frightfully embarrassed, I laid the completed project down beside his desk and looked for a seat. I would have turned around and walked out the same door I'd come in, had I not felt another seizure coming on. I spied an empty chair, sat down and lowered my face and head. Painful tears fell and I used my sweater sleeve to muffle the sounds of crying and collect the mucous pouring out of my nose. Son of a bitch, how dare he ask me questions about my life when he didn't even know me? I didn't know the meaning of the word 'saga' but from the flagrant arrogance in his voice, I knew it wasn't nice.

After about ten minutes I managed to collect myself enough to quietly get up and leave the room. The bathroom was just across the hall from the classroom. Once inside, I let all the emotion of failure rip out of me. I regained consciousness sometime later, on the cold tile floor with a roll of toilet paper lying next to me. Fuck me; another grand mal seizure must have occurred.

In the beginning of October the band left for Europe and I did my best to muddle through English 101, Mechanical Drawing,

Architectural Drafting and an art class. Not wanting to spend my 21st birthday alone, I flew to Baltimore and had dinner with Susan and her boyfriend at a swanky restaurant. I felt like an idiot. I was failing in school and I knew it. I wasn't in Paris with Joey and Lord only knows what the hell he was up to and now I'm driving a dark blue Mercedes four door sedan so my ass doesn't get in trouble. Joey had traded in the pretty white Corvette for a more "conservative" car. His dad was right: I hated it. I didn't give a damn about the prestige, German engineering of it, or the way people looked at me while driving the huge thing. My spirit, longing to be free, felt like an old married lady out to flaunt her stuff and the Eagles weren't coming to the rescue,

> *"She's got a Mercedes Benz,*
> *She's got a lot of pretty, pretty boys that she calls friends…"*

In November, before the three sold-out shows at The Boston Garden, Circus magazine came out with Joey's phone interview he had given them in March, admitting that for the first time in his life he was in love – from the tips of his toes to the tips of his hair.

> *"Much of his happiness is the result of a woman, Nancy Carlson.*
> *She made me realize a lot of heavy things about myself. Falling in*
> *love also gave me confidence. I've been living with my old lady for*
> *two years now and neither one of us has the desire to get married.*
> *But as long as we both feel this way we'll stay together. Besides*
> *the band, it's the only thing that has had meaning for me."*

The article in "Circus" was old news now but it said to the world that we didn't want to be married. I was hurt and didn't like that the rest of the world didn't know that we were looking at marriage, however discreetly, indiscreet we'd been. We'd both been secretly cheating and following the rules of the road, right?

The world was warped out of time and the merry-go-round had spun off its Peruvian coked base. Trains were jumping tracks and colliding as Steven and Joe continued to feud and cock fight about who had the best blow and the biggest balls to run the band. Nasty stuff... How the hell do you stay normal in a five ring circus when half the talent can't find the ring?

Three sold-out shows at home, The Boston Garden, good press coverage, everyone was happy. At an extravagantly supplied, lap of luxury meet and greet before the show on November 13th, one of the local newspapers was interviewing Joe Perry with Joey and I standing beside him. Joe Perry's mom, recently widowed and Joe's sister were beside us. The stupid, insensitive and intrusive reporter was asking Joe about his marriage to Elyssa and the loss of his father. What business was it of theirs? Joe's mom and sister looked really uncomfortable hearing the reporters get the story and ask whatever-you-like questions.

Joey piped up before Joe finished his brief comment and said as he hijacked my free hand, "Yeah, we're getting married too. I'm buying some land in New Hampshire and we're gonna tie the knot soon."

You fool, you haven't even asked me yet! All you've done is talk about it.

Spotlight seeking disaster and a botched proposal of marriage, I'm so done.

"You better shape up
Cause I need a man
And my heart is set on you
You better shape up
You better understand
To my heart I must be true..."

The damned merry-go-round wheeled base was also in desperate need of some serious 'Grease.'

Without further ado, the boys went back on the road again. Tom told Terry that they'd been to a huge diamond discount center and everyone bought gifts to bring home. Terry and I both wondered if

Mr. Kramer had purchased an engagement ring. When they got home, Joey put the gift bags away in the small bedroom and Terry and I took a little peek. There was a small gift wrapped ring box with the letter, 'N' on it and another slightly larger box. We were so excited, believing that Joey was going to man up and finally officially ask me to marry him. Terry and I both could hardly wait until he gave it to me with a big, fat Joey moment.

When I opened the box it was difficult to hide my disappointment. The ring box had an opal ring in it, my birthstone, and wasn't I happy that he remembered. I tried to be. The larger box contained a diamond necklace with an obvious, dark flaw inside the stone. I wasn't ungrateful, just confused and seemingly out of time with the rhythm in Joey's heart.

I was way behind at school and took an incomplete grade for my four classes, meaning that the college would grant me additional time, at any time, to complete the courses. I'd been failing early in the semester and then, just before finals, Joey neglected to put my suitcase in the car when we'd visited Mom. He left the bag sitting on the curb beside Mom's house. We called her from the airport when we realized what'd happened but it was too late, the suitcase was gone with all the schoolwork I'd brought with me to work on. Sadly, some of the beautiful clothes and lovely French perfume Joey had bought me in Paris were gone too.

We flew Mom up to Boston for the ginormous New Year's Eve Party we had at The Aerosmith Wherehouse. I was proud to have such a youthful looking acting mom to introduce to everyone. She was a highlight of the party and held her own with the bad boys of rock. I showed her how to recreationally snort the finest Peruvian flaked cocaine with a hundred dollar bill and toast the night away with Dom Perignon. As with most things in life, she did it well and was a fast learner.

We invited Tom, Terry, and Steven back to our apartment for breakfast. Steven brought a few others but I couldn't tell you who they were as I had to cook. I was really nervous about making fried eggs so as Steven was peering in to the refrigerator to grab the eggs

I asked him if he would help me. He told me he knew the secret to making perfectly fried eggs. He showed me how to get the pan ready with butter and carefully crack the eggs into the pan. When it's time to flip them over, you cheat. You add a little water to the pan, cover it with a lid and steam the little suckers for just a minute. No yoke breaking flipping required! Thank you, Steven.

After the late night breakfast, Joey and I went to bed leaving Mom and Steven in the den. I have no idea what time Steven left and I never did ask my mom about it.

As we were falling asleep with our bodies comfortably spooned, Joey mumbled over my shoulder,

"You're gonna marry me, right?"

Track **6**

WRITE ME A LETTER – A Treasure Chest

"**N**anny Goat," is the childhood nickname given to me by my mother. Joey adopted it.

This is the ten page letter, in its original form, that Joey had waiting for me when I returned home from the Johns Hopkins Hospital.

Up until now, it has been a treasure in a secret place that I've kept locked away, somewhere in my heart.

I share this with you with the intent that it opens your heart to the many complexing facets of love and youth.

I wish that I'd been able at the time to let this bold, beautiful and extremely raw expression of love into my heart and believe it.

I don't doubt that he meant every single word of it.

See transcript below.

Thurs.
June 3, 76

Nan —

There are many things in my life
now which are <u>very</u> <u>important</u>. I
suppose most of all is my <u>career</u> — even
though it gives me the most grief of
anything! I am grateful for everything
that happens to me — good — bad — indiff!
One of my most important subjects is
Nan — she's in the hospital — I
am <u>very</u>, <u>very</u> concerned about her
well being & weather she will be
O.K. or not. I don't think she is telling me all that is going on inside —
I want to know everything — but I
won't press the issue — she should do
whatever she thinks is right for herself.
I want her to have everything she
wants — and deserves — but, I want
it for her so badly — it causes us to
fight etc. . . . . sometimes I don't —
feel that she realizes this. I would
do anything for her. Anything !!!
My career dominates my life "for now"!
If people close to me, who know me
only understood how much I

long for & desire their way of life —
to be normal & be involved with
people — rather than a set of
drums or a dream — sure — its a dream
come true — but now, what
I must put up with this thing —
which to me is almost nothing
now — a grind — a bore — but
every one needs the money & this
is my way to it — I don't like it
as much as I used to — but of
coarse I'll do it — & take advantage
of it for what its worth — why not.
I deserve it — 12 years — & now it
starts to pay off — I love dad —
nan — etc — because they understand whats happening — & it's
hard for them — but they do it
only because of me — I'm part
of it — how hard is it for me!
Harder than you think everyone —
It would be real easy to quit!
Real easy!!!. But I'd flip out 5 yrs.
from now — so I'll stick it out.

why? because I've invested my
life in a dream - it hasn't
turned out ideally, but, what
the fuck - can't have everything,
can't have it all? - wrong -
I have it all - everything - and
I'm grateful - I just can't
show the way I want - I can't
tell anyone how much I feel
for them - I'm afraid? But even
if I am, I still feel what I
feel - and its real - the only true
judge is me - my way - & how I
am! Do I love you? - You know!
If you don't know, then you don't
know me - not many do! - not
even my dad - I love him so
very dearly - but he doesn't really
know me - for real - not as well
as Nancy dos, or my mom - maybe
that's why I choose to be closer to
him - than my mom - maybe she
knows me to well - I love her -
God knows she knows me

so well it's scary! Nan too!
Patty too - sometimes! Mostly my
mom & Nan! Nan is to smart for
her own good - she's so on the ball
she avoids herself - I'm very worried
about her health - Sometimes I feel
as though I'm the only one she really
really has - bottom line - she does
have me all the way - I just want
to make her realize she can do
everything herself - I want her to
realize so bad - sometimes I risk our
whole relationship to make her see a
certain way - only because I love
her so very, very much - otherwise
I wouldn't do anything - why
should I care - no one could ever
ever take her place - no one ever !!!
Nancy is the only person in the whole
world who really honestly &
truly understands me - for what
I am and what I do, & how I
conduct myself - She can always
deal and handle me - no matter

so what! — Thats a once in a
life time thing & I'm not giving it
up for anything or anyone —
There are many things to mak one
happy — if one is financially secure —
I never have to worry about money
and I never will — have to — but —
something like my goat is one of
those things you can't buy — no matter
how much you have —. I know I
complain & bitch about things —
thats human nature — anything
good & worthwhile must be worked
at — and the lord knows that
we have worked and suffered &
bled for what we have. And
in the long run we will not
only have each other — but we
will understand why & not too
many people do — life is a real
real full time career — & one
must be ready to conquer
it ! & rule his or her small
part — but, boy when you

know whats going on all the time, you really know. & & why guess at life, it only happens once – so – do it the best way possible – for Real –

Thanks Nanny –
for helping me get to whats really ~~so~~ real – more than anyone else – who thought they knew!

I only hope I helped to show you as much as you did me.

" All my love to you forever & ~~and~~ ever".

Joey

→

over

Nan— you must ~~be~~ realize ~~that~~
that ~~to~~ there has never been a
source of energy in my life anywhere near as strong or even stronger
than _myself_ — Never! and you
are— you offer more of AN POSITIVE ~~an~~ energy
source to me than EVER even my career —
because, my career ~~is~~ is established
& I'm living it out— weather its a
dream or not— it is real now — and
so are you, except you are so very
strong in your own way — & I'm
accustomed to being able to manipulate everything & anything having
to do with me. But not you! instead of
making you what I wanted — which is
what I was used to — I had to
deal & accept you for you! Which
put me through a change! The only
change I made myself ~~to~~ go through
that I was happy with. I know I've
been acting strange lately, (so have
you) I think it is because I'm
not sure or almost frightened of

90

what I really, really feel —
for you — I've never had the feeling
before — I don't know what it's all
about — when I dreamed about
doing what I'm doing now at age
14 & 15 — the dream never included
anyone but myself — but here I am
doing what I'm doing & loving it.
You changed the course of my whole
life & all my plans for myself. I never
thought about falling in love — or
sharing my dream or my life with
someone else — who would take
it, or me seriously? No one I knew!
Then there was Nancy — I sit here in
our home alone — with myself —
Expressing myself — for real — something
I haven't done for a long time!
Most likely too long — But even
when I did do it, it was only
to read over myself — for no one else.
But, this, I intend for you to read.
Yes, I'm very very stoned — but this is
real Nan — and if I never tell you again

these pages tell only truth. A lot of
it because you're not here & I miss
you so very much — even if I don't
say so out loud — I've always
been able to express myself better by
writing than speaking — and the
urge over came me tonite — so here
I'am — The main reason I couldn't
sleep is cause of you — if anything
is seriously wrong with you I'll
be really sleepless — being here by
myself is not really being home —
I'm lonely; alone —, and a piece of
me is missing, Honest Nan — I know
I can't speak these words — but its
better that I write them then not
say them at all.
     I would only go to N.Y. to
be with my family & Jerry. so I
wouldn't have to be ~~so~~ alone. If
the choice ever came — I would miss
you a lot more than my family,
even my father, and you know
how much I love them all.

Sometimes I even think I _hate you_.
Know why? because you know me
so well – to well! You know ~~even~~
what I'll do or say in just about
any given situation. That can
really scare a person – & it can also
make a person feel something thats
indiscribable. You make me feel both
those feelings ~~all the time~~ very often.
It's now 7:30 AM. I'm going to sleep –
I sure hope you come home soon!
I miss you very much!!!
                    Joey.

I miss youre posative energy!

When youre ~~even~~ here its so
Prevelent, that I take it for
granted. But, now that youre
not here – everything is so nuetral

Nancy Karlson Bridge

Thurs.

June 3, 1976

Nan –
(Page 1)

    There are many things in my life now which are <u>very important</u>. I suppose most of all is my <u>career</u> – even though it gives me the most grief of anything! I am <u>grateful</u> for everything that happens to me – good – bad – indiff. One of my most important subjects is Nan – she's in the hospital – I am <u>very, very</u> concerned about her well being and weather she will be O.K. or not. I don't think that she is telling me all that is going on inside – I want to know everything – but I won't press the issue – she should do whatever she thinks is right for herself. I want her to have everything she wants – and deserves –but, I want it for her so badly – it causes us to fight etc….sometimes I don't – feel that she realizes this. I would do anything for her. Anything!!! My career dominates my life for now! If people close to me, who know me only understood how much I

(Page 2)

    long for & desire their way of life – to be normal & be involved with people – rather than a set of drums or a dream – sure – it's a dream come true – but <u>now</u> what I must put up with this thing – which to me is almost nothing now – a grind – a bore – but everyone needs the money & this is my way to it – I don't like it as much as I used to – but of course I'll do it - & take advantage of it for what it's worth – why not. I deserve it – 12 years and now it starts to pay off – I love dad – Nan –etc – because they understand what's happening - & it's hard for them – but they do it only because of me – I'm part of it – how hard it is for me! Harder than you think everyone – It would be really easy to quit! Real easy!!! But I'd flip out 5 yrs from now – so I'll stick it out.

(Page 3)

Why? Because I've invested my life in a dream – it hasn't turned out ideally, but, what the fuck – can't have everything. Can't have it all? – wrong – I have it all – everything – and I'm grateful – I just can't show it the way I want – I can't tell anyone how much I feel for them – I'm afraid? But even if I am afraid I still feel what I feel – and it's real – the only true judge is me – my way - & I know how I am! Do I love you? – You know! If you don't know, then you don't know me – not many do! – Not even my dad – I love him so very dearly – but he doesn't really know me – for real – not as well as Nancy does, or my mom – maybe that's why I choose to be closer to him – than my mom – maybe she knows me too well – I love her – God knows she knows me

(Page 4)

so well it's scary! Nan too! Patty too – sometimes! Mostly my mom and Nan! Nan is too smart for her own good – she's so on the ball she avoids herself – I'm very worried about her health – Sometimes I feel as though I'm the only one she has – bottom line – she does have me all the way – I just want to make her realize she can do everything herself – I want her to realize so bad – sometimes I risk our whole relationship to make her see a certain way – only because I love her so very, very much – otherwise I wouldn't do anything – why should I care – no-one could ever take her place. No one ever!!! Nancy is the only person in the whole world who really honestly & truly understands me – for what I am and what I do, & how I conduct myself – She can always deal and handle me – no matter

(Page 5)

what! – That's a once in a lifetime thing & I'm not giving it up for anything! Or anyone – There are many things to make one happy – if one is financially secure – I never have to worry about money and I never will – have to – but – something like my goat is one of those things you can't buy – no matter how much you have – I know I complain & bitch about things – that's human nature – anything good & worthwhile must be worked at – and the Lord knows that we have worked and suffered & bleed

95

*for what we have. And in the long run we will not only have each other –
but we will understand why & not too many people do – life is a <u>real, real</u>
full time career - & one must be ready to conquer it! & rule his or her small
part – but, boy when you*

(Page 6)

*know what's going on all the time, you really know & why guess at life,
it only happens once – so – do it the best way possible – for Real –*
Thanks Nanny –
*For helping me to get to what's really real – maybe more than anyone
else – who though they knew!*
I only hope I helped to show you as much as you did me.

*"All My love to you
forever & ever."*
<u>*Joey*</u>

Over

(Page 6)

*Nan – you must realize that there has never been a source of energy
in my life anywhere near as strong or even stronger than <u>myself.</u> – Never!
And you are – you offer more of a positive energy source to me than even
my career – because, my career is established & I'm living it out – weather
it's a dream or not – it is real now – and so are you, except that you are so
very strong in your own way - & I'm accustomed to being able to manipulate
everything and anything having to do with me. But not you! Instead of
making you what I wanted – which is what I was used to – I had to deal
with and accept you for you! Which put me through a change! The only
change I ever made myself go through that I was happy with. I know I've
been acting strange lately (so have you) I think it is because I'm not sure or
almost frightened of*

(Page 7)

What I really, really feel – for you – I've never had the feeling before – I don't know what's it's all about – when I dreamed about doing what I'm doing at age 14 & 15 – the dream never included anyone but myself – but here I am doing what I'm doing & loving it. You changed the course of my whole life & and all my plans for myself. I never thought about falling in love – or sharing my dream or my life with someone else – who would take it or me seriously? No one I knew! Then there was Nancy – I sit here in our home alone – with myself – Expressing myself – for real – something I haven't done for a long time! Most likely too long – But even when I did do it, it was only to read over myself – for no one else. But, this, I intend for you to read. Yes, I'm very stoned – but this is real Nan – and if I never tell you again

(Page 8)

These pages tell only truth. A lot of it because you're not here & I miss you so very much – even if I don't say so out loud – I've always been able to express myself better by writing than speaking – and the urge came over me tonight – so here I am – The main reason I couldn't sleep is cause of you – if anything is seriously wrong with you I'll really be sleepless – being here by myself is not really being home – I'm lonely: alone -, and a piece of me is missing, Honest Nan – I know I can't speak these words – but it's better that I write them than not say them at all.

I would only go to NY to be with my family & Jerry so I wouldn't have to be alone. If the choice ever came I would miss you a lot more than my family, even my father, and you know how much I love them all.

(Page 9)

Sometimes I even think I hate you. Know why? Because you know me so well – too well! You know what I'll do or say in just about any given situation. That can really scare a person – & it can also make a person feel

97

something that's indescribable. You make me feel both those feelings very often.

It's now 7:30 am. I'm going to sleep – I sure hope you come home soon! I miss you very much!!!

Joey

I miss your positive energy! When you're here it's so prevalent that I take it for granted. But, now that you're not here – everything is so neutral.

When you stop racking up the frequent flyer miles, I will too, is what I told my young-ass self. Mindless sex doesn't mean anything, right?

We were being consumed by the toxic and twisted road to hell of fame and fortune. We'd slacked on our three-week agreement of seeing each other and I was beginning to take it personally. Joey flew me out to the last leg of the Rocks US Tour, 1976.

Track **7**

BUNNIES, BABES & A
BAND ONBOARD

Okay, I'll bite. Something's wrong. What in heaven's name could possibly be wrong this early in the morning? We had just boarded a small chartered plane somewhere in the fields of the Midwest and none of us or the sun had been up for very long. It was a grey and bleak early winter morning and the sound of the plane's engine, ready for take-off, only amplified the ringing in my ears from the band's concert the night before.

Spotting two seats together on the left front side of the plane, I began to make my way toward them when Joey, with his carry-on luggage, pushed his way in front of me to grab the window seat.

"Move, I want the window", Joey grumbled.

Jeez, I thought, you do this for a living, fly everywhere, always having the seat of your choice, will it really bother you that much if I have the window seat this time?

Stunned by his lack of politeness or manners in that moment, I stepped aside allowing him to plop himself down next to the window.

"I don't even want to look at him," Joey said.

It was way too early in the morning to try and wrap my tired brain around why Joey was acting this way or who he didn't want to look at. He'd been angry and withdrawn the night before when we went to bed and woke up with the same foul attitude.

"Oh, sit down" he beefed again. "We're about to take off."

After fastening my seatbelt I closed my eyes, thankful that I had remembered to remove last night's mascara and was hopeful of going back to sleep. I didn't want to wake up and try to figure out why Joey was in such a pre-pubescent snit.

"He's jeopardized the whole band" Joey ranted while fumbling to fasten his seatbelt. "Fucking Steven – he's really fucking done it this time."

Realizing that Joey's anger wasn't going to dissipate anytime soon, I opened my eyes to look back at Steven. Steven Tyler and his lady friend, Bebe Buell, were snuggled in the last two seats on the right side of the plane. I didn't see the problem, other than the fact that Steven probably still had a girlfriend back in Boston, which never seemed to bother Joey before.

"Everybody's pissed at Steven", he continued to spout. I looked around the plane and saw the Aerosmith entourage of band members, managers, wives and girlfriends secured in their seats and ready for take-off. No one seemed upset or in a tirade like Joey; many were already sleeping or well on their way to peaceful slumber. I noticed that a few people had ear plugs on – why hadn't I thought of that? My eyes were begging to close again to relieve the sandpaper feeling in them of not having had enough sleep.

"Shit, man. I can't fucking believe it. He's really done it now. Look at him." Joey spoke louder now to be heard above the roar of the plane's engine during take-off.

After the plane reached its cruising altitude I turned around for a second glance and saw an image of something that I knew I'd never forget. Steven and Bebe were nestled in the last two seats on the plane both wearing over-sized high collared fur coats. They were snuggling, laughing, whispering to each other and playfully teasing one another seemingly lost in the bliss of their own little world. I couldn't hear what they were saying but their laughter now was louder than the gentle hum of the plane's engine which seemed to aggravate Joey even more.

"Look at that. You see that? And, she's Playboy's Miss November!" Joey huffed.

What did it matter that Bebe had posed for a centerfold in Playboy Magazine in 1974, almost three years before? I was a Playboy Bunny in Boston and now found myself wanting to defend the hutch against a mean predator. Joey was so angry that his cheeks were flushed and his sweet blue eyes were beginning to bulge. It wasn't like him to get this worked up over anything and I was half afraid that if I took the bait and asked what was wrong he might explode and take the whole plane down with him.

For the good of everyone onboard I took the bait and asked him what the hell was wrong. What could this sweet, lady charming, lizard-catching outdoor boy at heart possibly have done to "piss off an entire plane of people" as Joey had protested?

"She's pregnant! We're fucked. The band's fucked." Joey offered as the steam from his pressure cooker of emotions began to release.

I didn't get it. I didn't see the problem. I turned around once more to fully embrace and take into my heart the memory of those two beautiful long haired, fur covered people, wrapped in love and lust and lost in a wondrous world of their own like a freshly shaken snow globe. I wanted to be in that world with them.

"Bebe is Todd Rundgren's girlfriend," Joey explained. "It's okay for Steven to do what he pleases with other women, but not a legendary musician like Todd. You don't mess with that. Todd's one of the guys we've looked up to in our careers and this mistake is gonna cost the band, big time." My heart ached for Joey as he said those words to me. How could he not see how in love and happy to be pregnant they were?

Unburdened now by the weight and intensity of the emotional baggage he'd been carrying, Joey closed his eyes and went to sleep. I was fully awake and aware that Steven and Bebe shared something that Joey and I were lacking; passion and a "who cares what the world thinks" way of being.

Where had our passion gone? Was I sure I still wanted to marry him and have his children? Was this a defining moment in our relationship or was Joey simply plagued with fear? I knew when we got back to Boston Joey would continue to ask me when we could go shopping for an engagement ring. He'd already asked me several times since New Year's Day to set a day when we could go shopping together for a ring.

I wanted him to do it himself, surprise me and give me a powerful moment of choice after his botched proposals. I felt like an item to be checked off on his insanely busy agenda. To me, every time he asked when we could go ring shopping, it felt like he was asking me to fill the gas tank or remember to pick up toilet paper.

And even though I loved him with all my heart, something unknown continued to pull at my soul and I was hesitant to commit to marrying him.

I closed my eyes and tried to sleep as Joey reached for and found my hand. Tears began to fill my tired eyes as I felt the warmth and strength of his strong fingers sliding between mine. He gently squeezed my hand twice and whispered, "I love you." I looked back once more at Steven and Bebe, quieter now, but still like two fur balls of unstoppable energy and noticed that she had the window seat.

It would be ten years before I realized just how special the moment I witnessed with Steven and Bebe was; the child she was carrying would become Liv Tyler.

When we got back to Boston, Joey seemed to have forgotten why he had been so angry with Steven and told me to pack for New Hampshire; we were going to visit Steven for a few days and to look at buying land near Steven's house in Lake Sunapee. I was glad that Joey's attention had shifted from buying me an engagement ring to purchasing land on which to build a log cabin home. I now had more time to consider becoming his wife.

As I packed, I tried not to think about the ambivalence that was beginning to take root in my heart concerning Joey. I only wanted the best for him and I couldn't ignore that 'something' was tugging at my soul, preventing me from saying 'yes' to marrying him. We'd been together for three years, shared three homes and had experienced a lot of growing up during that time. I didn't want to make the same mistakes in love that I'd seen my parents make, but I'd already made a huge one and didn't even realize it.

Joey had been unfaithful to me and my defense mechanism was to fire back secretly with affairs of my own. I'm not proud of it; I didn't know any better at the time. It's what I'd seen my parents do. In having secret affairs of my own I reasoned that I could never be hurt again if Joey strayed. I'd built a wall around my heart and it seemed to work, for a while.

Now that Joey was planning the rest of our lives together; expecting that I would marry him and live in a log cabin home with him in New Hampshire, my moment of truth was quickly approaching. It never occurred to me that I had done anything wrong by being unfaithful or that I had anything to confess. Honestly, at twenty-one years old, I believed that this was how people in relationships survived the heartaches of being in love.

The tug at my soul was that I wanted more from life than just being Joey's wife and living my life around his life. I knew that there was something that I could do extremely well – I just didn't know what it was.

I finished packing and we headed north to New Hampshire arriving at the home of Henry and Gail Smith just after lunchtime. Henry was a longtime friend of Steven's and a remarkable roadie and manager for rock bands. I didn't know at the time that he'd been Led Zeppelin's road manager; I just knew he was a down to earth nice guy. We were to be his house guests for two nights.

Henry came out to meet us as we pulled up and I remember opening the car door and smelling fresh green pine from the tall trees that surrounded his beautiful log cabin home. The sky was abundantly blue with only a few puffy white clouds hovering over the cabin. Henry and Joey hugged like two long lost loggers before we went inside. As Henry opened the front door we were greeted by the smell of bread baking in the oven. Henry said we'd picked a good weekend to visit; they were calling for twenty inches of snow.

Henry called Steven to let him know we'd arrived and then showed us the house. It was open and spacious with windows positioned in just the right places to allow for maximum sunlight to enter. The master bedroom had become the room just off to the right of the kitchen as Gail was having trouble with her pregnancy and was restricted to bed rest. There was a loft upstairs where Joey and I would stay that first night. It was clear to me by the loving tidiness – everywhere – and the special touches of flowers and frills that Gail had not stayed in bed. She seemed happy to see people and have guests in her home in the woods.

Steven burst through the front door like a roaring ball of light obviously happy to have more friends to play with on what would become a snow stopping New England weekend. I hardly recognized him in his blue jeans, boots and short sleeved white t-shirt. His hair was a sexy mess, he was coatless and right at home in the backwoods of Lake Sunapee. Any female who says she doesn't find Steven Tyler attractive is either lying or dead.

"Whadaya wanna do first? Ski, hike, shoot guns – have you kids had lunch? How was the trip? It's gonna snow ya know. Gail, whatcha got to eat? Joey, where ya lookin' for land? Who's goin' whitcha? Henry, did ya get my whatjamacallit back yet?" We all laughed as Steven rapid-fired the contents of his ever-loving mind around Gail's kitchen table. No casualties, just rip-roaring laughter from the crowd of four.

Never having been on skis of any kind, I opted for cross country skiing through the woods with Steven. He assured me I wouldn't need a coat; we were gonna get sweaty. Joey, Gail and Henry watched from the window as Steven and I began our trek. About twenty feet into the snowy woods I realized how tall and dense the trees were and wondered where I might end up if I continued to follow him. I turned around and headed back toward the cabin.

I heard Steven shout from behind me, "Hey, ever shot a gun before?"

What kind of question was that, of course I hadn't.

"Hey, wanna shoot a gun?" He's got to be kidding.

"Wait up, I've got a gun in my Jeep, I'll show ya how."

Dear Lord in heaven, let me get these things off my feet and get into the house. Steven, having un-strapped his skis before me, went to his Jeep and grabbed what looked to me like a sawed-off shotgun.

Putting the gun in to my hand Steven said, "Here. I'll show you how to hold it. Just hold it like this…"

"No! I don't want to hold that thing!" I cried out.

Steven took the gun and shot it straight up into the air.

Henry and Joey came running from the house and Joey shouted, "What the fuck are you doing man?"

"I'm teachin' your lady how to shoot!" Steven defended.

"Yeah, well be careful she doesn't shoot you! Put that thing away. Are you nuts?" Joey fired back.

Steven told Joey if we were going to live in New Hampshire that I should know how to shoot a gun. Joey acquiesced, "Okay, just one time. Straight up; be careful, Nan."

I held it with both hands and shot directly into the sky, almost falling back into the snow. Truthfully, it was exhilarating until I remembered Newton's theory of relativity that what goes up must come down. I handed the gun back to Steven hoping I hadn't killed a rabbit or any other woodland creature.

We went back into the house and Henry and Joey continued their conversation about buying land in New Hampshire. Steven had a hard time sitting down or staying in one place for very long. He seemed to be moving like a 78 speed vinyl record when the rest of us were moving at a slower 45 speed. It didn't take long for Steven to get bored with the prospecting land talk and leave.

Joey and I enjoyed a wonderful country supper with Henry and Gail and did what most people do in that part of the country; went to bed early. From the guestroom loft upstairs I could see down over the living room and beyond it through the downstairs windows. Night brought a very quiet still to the woods and it was beginning to snow, making everything seem blanketed with soundproof walls. We fell into a deep sleep and woke up to the smell of breakfast cooking and soft light streaming through the windows. I was bear-cold and Joey told me to put my boots on before heading downstairs to the kitchen. It was then that I realized I wouldn't need all the clothes, make-up and curlers I'd brought with me. Nor would I be re-polishing my nails anytime soon. The only thing needed here was a warm smile of gratitude to share with our hosts.

Breakfast with Henry and Gail brought cultural insight as to how life in New Hampshire might be for Joey and me: a slower paced, cold outside but cozy inside, good neighbors and friends, real jam making, safe, secure, fat and happy and eventually pregnant with child. It was romantic.

Joey was certain that he wanted this ever-after bliss of a life for us. He wanted to take us as far away from Boston, New York and the insanity of the rock and roll fortune and fame business as he could get us. He often said, "Get the fuck out of the city, as far away as we possibly can." It was his mantra at the time.

I saw the life he described for us as being a place where I would be held prisoner and hostage from my own dreams. Not yet having the voice of wisdom and understanding, all I saw was a painful love-trap that I didn't want to step into. The closer Joey got to me the more I wanted to pull away. I didn't trust love and it felt as if my personal survival was at stake.

I helped Henry and Gail clean the kitchen as Joey made a phone call to confirm the sites where he'd be going to look at land. Joey hung up the phone and asked Henry if he thought there was any wiggle room on price negotiation. Henry said, probably; he personally knew most of the sellers. Joey asked if I'd mind staying behind in case Gail needed anything while the men went to do their bidding; I could see the properties later. Henry tucked Gail into bed under a handmade quilt and kissed her goodbye.

I went into the living room and turned on the television. An Elvis Presley movie, "GI Blues" was on, followed by "The Buddy Holly Story." Being a child of the fifties and sixties, I enjoyed the heck out of them both. The music made me feel alive and happy inside. When Henry and Joey returned I was as giddy as a six year old and Gail was still napping. Joey said it went well and we were buying land.

Joey wanted to give Henry and his sleeping wife some alone time so we headed over to Steven's for the evening. Steven was still a live wire when we got there. Pointing to the pizza boxes and soda bottles on his dining room table he said he hoped we could stay for dinner. Bottles of alcohol were on the table too and Joey poured himself a tall celebratory drink. There were many closed doors in Steven's house with people I didn't know going in and out. I think his girlfriend Julia may have been there, but I didn't see her. Joey was in and out of the rooms, refreshing his drink each time. I trusted Joey, and that whatever was going on behind those closed doors, I didn't need to know about. I assumed it was the consumption of drugs.

I was content to watch the snow fall and fall and fall. I'd never seen so much snow in my life.

Hours passed and when I went to look for Joey, Steven found me wandering about his house. He opened the door to the room where Joey had passed out and suggested that I let him sleep it off. Closing the door, Steven, still wide awake but not seemingly stoned, high or drunk like Joey said, "Hey! I know what we can do now, let's drive across the lake!"

From the look on my face he must have known that I thought he was truly off his rocker. He added, "It's safe. It's frozen over this time of year. People do it all the time – there are even races across it. Come on, it'll be fun."

Why on earth I got into that Jeep with him I'll never know. The other guys in the band always joked about what a bad driver Steven was. Seeing the kitchen lights on at Henry and Gail's, Steven suggested we stop by and say hello, at one in the morning. As he drove the Jeep up and onto the front lawn, he neglected to push the clutch in before stopping to park and we were jilted forward, almost banging our heads on the windshield. Gail, laughing, opened the front door with a warm, lighthearted smile and asked what we were up to. Steven told her, just a little night driving across the lake, and asked if she had anything to eat.

"Yes, of course, come on in" Gail replied, still chuckling. "You're funny. You're gonna drive Joey's girlfriend across the lake in the middle of the night? It's still snowing, Steven. I don't think it's a good idea and some people say the lake may not be frozen all the way through."

"Ah, sure it is. We'll be fine. Whatcha got to eat?" The hungry lad continued, "Something we can take with us."

Gail made Jiffy Pop popcorn for us, swirling the pan around and around by the handle on top of the stove until the foil package expanded tall and wide. "Where's Joey?" she asked in a pleasant tone.

I told her that he'd had a little too much to drink while celebrating his choice to become a New Hampshire resident – a liberated man in the woods.

Steven and I took the popcorn and Gail's blessing to have a good time and be safe as we headed for the lake. It was spooky dark with who knows what kind of nocturnal creatures stirring in wait at the edge of the lake. I opened the cooled down popcorn and Steven and I ate it by the handfuls as we sat in quiet anticipation, a few feet from the lake.

"Ready?" he asked.

Breaking the silence of my internal dialogue, wondering if he would try to kiss me, I said, "Ready!"

Steven put the Jeep in first gear and gunned it. We went about ten feet onto the lake before we started to sink.

"Ut-oh, we gotta go back, it's not frozen." Steven muttered.

No shit, Sherlock. Get us out of here, I prayed. Steven tried several times to put the Jeep in reverse gear, failing on each attempt.

"Where the hell's reverse on this thing?" he said, again to himself.

We were going down and for as much as I wondered what it might be like to kiss Steven Tyler, I certainly wasn't prepared to drown with him. No, I will not sink; I will not die here in this vehicle with him. I reached across grabbed the gear shift and told him to push in the clutch. I put the Jeep in reverse and told him to back up now – slow and easy. Thank God he took direction well and we made it safely back to the shore.

Happy to be alive, we drove back to his house where Joey was awake and worried sick about where we'd been. Joey called Steven a few choice names and admonished me for going off with him in the first place. Joey said without hesitation that we were leaving as soon as the sun came up.

Steven said that would be impossible because it was no longer twenty inches of snow in the forecast, there was a blizzard headed our way.

Joey said, "Watch me."

We left early in the morning before anyone was up in Steven's house and stopped by Henry and Gail's to pick up our things. By the grace of God and at a very slow speed, we made it to the highway. It was nuts – we were in the Porsche, driving through a blizzard to get back to Boston early because Joey was pissed. It took most of the day to get home driving at twenty miles per hour in scary, white-out conditions. That's a long time to be in a car with someone who's mad at you.

Our apartment was cold and dark when we got home and Joey's temperament was unchanged. If he was scared that I could have been hurt by my adventure with Steven he didn't say so. He just offered me his back when we got in bed.

A few days later, after speaking to each other only when necessary, Steven stopped by. He and Joey talked behind closed doors in our den and I stayed in the bedroom. When Steven was leaving, Joey called to me from the hallway and asked that I come out and tell our guest goodbye. I could tell that everything was peaceful now because Joey was smiling, laughing and twirling a curl in his long blond hair with his fingers. Like a once scolded puppy I timidly came out of the bedroom and walked toward them. They were both smiling in agreement as I approached.

"It's okay, Nan. I'm sorry. I love this guy and I forgot I could trust him. You didn't do anything wrong." Joey's words of praise and forgiveness brought huge smiles to all three of us. As I walked Steven to the door and hugged him goodbye, he whispered in my ear, "He fucking loves your ass. Be good."

Bored and Lonely

Sexy New Love

Old Fashioned Badge Making

My Drummer Boy

Joey's Article
Circus Magazine
November 25, 1975

Different Drummer

Why Aerosmith's Joey Kramer Is Media Shy

by Oneida Bell

Joey Kramer doesn't do interviews. He doesn't dig them. He avoids them. Joey likes his privacy, even though he's the drummer in Aerosmith, which is fast becoming the biggest band in America. Joey takes a low profile. He wants to be like Charlie Watts who can still walk into most restaurants and order dinner without getting served up a mass of cloying, screaming fans. Kramer believes being famous has its drawbacks—the media monster devours flesh and blood people and pukes out plastic inflatable images.

"I think it's all suspense," declares Joey Kramer in a one-of-a-kind interview with Circus magazine. "I'm not trying to live a longer life, I mean, I'm not trying to be something I'm not, to project an image, I consider myself to be a pretty normal, regular person and so I don't like to exploit myself by projecting something else . . . If you let them they'll push you right out in the middle of the street naked.

"When you get right down to it," Kramer delves, "all we are, are people that other people who aren't into the kids, whoever—they're just look-

ing for something to relate to as heavy that they make as something that we're not. Once you start to believe that, once you start to tell a lie long enough, you start to believe it—and that's how these guys start projecting images. The people I admire are the ones who are the biggest stars, but who keep themselves together."

O.K., then who is the real, regular guy called Joe Kramer? What are the facts? Will the official Aerosmith bio, compiled by Leber/Krebs, Aerosmith's management, help? It says: "Joey was born in the Bronx

CIRCUS MAGAZINE 55

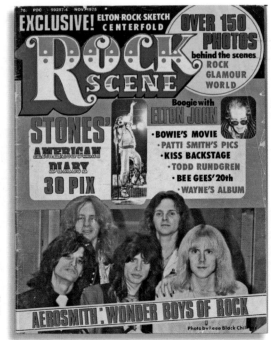

Cover Rock Scene Magazine
November, 1975

A Long Stone Jetty—Cape Cod

A Sad Little World

Galley Wench and Recovering My Dreams

Miami Beach, Florida

Track 8

LET FREEDOM RING – Leaving the Cenacle Behind

Was this just a phase Joey was going through?

Was I certain that I no longer wanted to marry him?

How could we restore communication and determine what was really going on?

Night after night while Joey was at home during pre-production on the next album, we barely spoke. We ate, watched a little TV and went to bed early. Our king-sized bed now seemed like an ocean of deep, dark water and inaudible words which would never reach the surface.

Joey needed his rest and the band needed to knock out another record. Our lives had become the success of Aerosmith and we were lost in a cold, dark sea of exhaustion, confusion and deceit. I was afraid to reach for him in the night and hold him as I once had. He was tormented by demons that I didn't fully understand and I didn't know how to help him.

He was angry, sad and scared. He questioned the love of his family, friends and even the fans. Did they really love him – or just his money? Did they still see who he was on the inside – or did they now see him as a rock idol?

Clearly the fans could only adore what they saw on stage – did they really love him or just the music?

Everyone was going through something – and none of us had our feet on the ground.

After I told Joey I didn't want to go "ring shopping" on Valentine's Day, 1977, as he had planned, he took my jewelry box and slung it down the long hallway in our apartment like a bowling ball, breaking the box and spilling its contents when it hit the wall.

I waited for him to leave the apartment and decided to just leave everything on the floor. If I cleaned up the mess, would he remember what he had done? I thought if I left everything where it had landed in the hallway – he might just explain his actions and tell me what was really going on inside his world, obscured from me.

It was dark outside when he returned home. He smiled, and cleaned up the mess. We ate, watched TV and went to bed, bodies a little closer.

Tom and Terry suggested a day trip to Cape Cod. It was a lovely ride with plenty of sunshine. When we got to the Cape, Joey refused to get out of the car. He just sat sadly in the backseat of Tom's car. Tom, Terry and I got out, walked around and took pictures of the Cape's long stone jetty.

Joey didn't want to shop or have lunch as we had planned. We couldn't coax him to get out of the car. We left him in the car while we got a bite to eat and then drove home to Boston. Looking back now, especially when I see the pictures of him slumped in the backseat of Tom's car, I can see that he was severely depressed. I didn't know at the time what depression was. I now understand that nothing I could have done would have made him happy.

I was lost as to how to help him and I knew marrying him wasn't the answer. I didn't see him being any happier if we were married and building our home together in Sunapee. What kept gnawing at my soul was a desperate feeling that I had to save myself. I did not want to live in this sad little world of his where I couldn't reach him or help him. I absolutely had to find myself and my place in this world.

I continued to support Joey as the band finished pre-production in Waltham and got ready to go to New York to continue recording the album at a place called "The Cenacle." The Cenacle was formerly a huge monastery in Armonk, New York, that the band's management rented and turned into a recording studio. I hoped that the change of scenery would do him good and looked forward to being alone to figure things out.

The morning that Joey left for New York he told me that there was way too much going on with the band and getting this album done and that I should not plan on visiting him there. He said it would take everything he had to 'remain sane and be locked up with those guys for six weeks.' Joey told me that it would be a miracle if they were able to finish this record.

It had been about two weeks since I'd seen him and still being on a leave of absence from the Playboy Club, I had the time I needed to contemplate what my life had become. I didn't want to go ring shopping or marry Joey, but I wasn't sure I wanted to leave him either.

I thought if I went to Baltimore – for the summer, while Joey was away – I could live with Susan, be around family and friends and work in my own hometown. I knew I needed to recover – me. I was no longer happy living in Joey's world. I wasn't looking forward to building a house in Sunapee, New Hampshire, on the recently purchased land. Living there seemed to me even more isolated than I already felt in heavily populated Boston.

Something was calling me and pulling on my spirit and I had to find out what it was. Being in Baltimore for the summer would allow me to be surrounded by people I knew in a big, small town and the familiarity of my old stomping ground. I desperately needed to reconnect with my heart. The only question was how to present the idea to Joey so that he'd be clear I wasn't leaving him – I just had to find me.

I had little hope of Joey being comfortable with the idea of me being away for the summer, especially living with Susan, but I hoped with all my heart that he would understand and trust the love I had for him.

Out of the blue, on a Thursday night, Dory Hamilton, a lady from Philadelphia who Steven occasionally saw, called me and asked if I would drive down to New York with her to visit the guys at The Cenacle. I told her that Joey had asked me not to visit and that I thought it best to respect his wishes. Dory chatted on like we were long lost girlfriends (we were not) and asked if she could stop by the apartment for a visit with me.

Dory, like my friend Susan from Baltimore who had dated Steven, had a way of putting people at ease and being down home comfortable with anyone. She was very interested in why I would honor Joey's request and not visit him. I tried to explain that I saw this as mutual support for what we were both up to – Joey remaining sane and on purpose to finishing the album and me – trying to determine what my life was truly about.

Dory was as charming as Steven, and convincing, if not seductive, that we, as powerfully budding young women, should be able to have it all.

"Go see your man. Surprise him! Tell him in person that you want to go home for the summer. Love him real good, seal it with a kiss and then go to Baltimore!"

She was persuasive – I remember wishing that she would talk to Joey for me so I wouldn't have to see the hurt in his eyes, fearing that I might not come back, when I told him about my idea.

We left for New York the next night in my car, around 9:00 p.m. Steven was expecting to see Dory; Joey had no idea I was coming. I was uneasy the whole way; I knew it wasn't right to surprise him this way after I'd agreed not to visit. When we arrived Dory was shown to Steven's room and I was taken to Joey's. The lights were out, the room was quiet and I could see Joey cocooned under a blanket on the right side of the bed. The light from the hallway with the door opening must have startled him because he quickly lifted his head off the pillow asked who was there.

When he realized it was me he said, "What the fuck, Nan! I told you not to come!"

From the depths of fear he shouted, "This is insane. What are you doing here? Tell me. Why did you come?"

I was too scared to move from the open doorway.

"Close the door. Get in here. What the fuck!" he yelled as he repositioned himself tightly back under the covers.

I quietly tiptoed in and gently put my travel bag down close to the door, knowing I would not be staying for long.

Unsure what to do next, as any uninvited guest would be, and wired from the late night drive, I spotted a chair and eased myself down not wanting to awaken the sleeping bear again.

"Get in bed. I can't sleep with you sitting there watching me." His instructions were clear but I was definitely not ready to climb in bed with him or pretend to be asleep with what I didn't understand.

I told him to go back to sleep and that I was going down to Steven and Dory's room for a while. He said nothing. I needed to tell someone I knew that I'd made a mistake in coming and was hoping for some sage advice. Steven and Dory saw it as no big deal. Their advice was to go back, get in bed with him and talk in the morning.

I went back, got in bed and felt the familiar cold back of his spine to me. Eyes closed, but both of us very much awake with minds racing, laid in the same position for about an hour.

Softer voice now, but still unhappy, Joey asked me again why I came after he had told me not to.

Wanting so badly to be heard, I told him about my idea of being in Baltimore for the summer.

"I don't want to spend one more hot summer in Boston, alone. I want to go to Baltimore, just for the summer, and I'll come back in September when you've finished the album."

"Where would you live – how would you live?" he questioned.

Afraid to tell him, and certain that he wouldn't be happy with my answer, I meekly replied, "I'll get a job and stay with Susan."

The dead silence returned and I remember last looking at the clock around 5:00 a.m. I woke up around 11:00 a.m. and Joey was gone. It didn't take long to find him; he was outside on the front driveway washing the new Ferrari.

Neither one of us spoke as I watched him wash the rear of the car. Water and soap suds filled the huge circular driveway. Joey didn't look at me until he came back to the front of the car where I was standing.

Holding the hose – now pointed toward the building – away from me and the car, Joey looked at me dead on and said, "You see this car? This car's worth forty fucking thousand dollars – what are you worth?"

Stunned, mouth gaping wide open, I could feel the spirit of my grandfather's stout, determined Masonic character rising up in me. I felt the heat in my face as my heart forced blood to the top of my head. Somewhere inside of me, I was aware of a small still voice telling me to speak softly now and choose my words carefully.

"Joey" – I began, with deep respect for this 'knowing' inside of me, pausing slightly to control my breath, but the prophetic words had to come out – "Joey, I hope it doesn't take you smacking up this car on the Mass Pike to show you a thing or two about where your priorities lie."

It was clear to me in that moment that Joey was really off his rocker now. I knew he had been distrusting his family and friend's motives for a while – questioning – did they really love him or his money? I got that, I thought I was helping him through this tumultuous time of doubt, self love and rapidly changing circumstances.

With the running hose still pointed at the ground and seemingly big guns in his mouth pointed right at me, Joey said, "Get out. Go back to Boston and get your shit out of my place."

Your place? Our home? What the hell has come over you?

I said nothing as I walked back inside The Cenacle with my self respect still intact. I wouldn't let him see how deeply his words had slain me; I wouldn't hemorrhage and bleed out on the pavement while short stuff continued to wash the vehicle in question. I made my way to Tom and Terry's room and once inside let all the tears and unspoken feelings about Joey release. I was crying so hard that Terry poured me a whiskey, sat down next to me and held me with both arms. She kept shushing me, rocking me and telling me that everything would be okay. I didn't know until then that she did possess strong maternal instincts.

Tom said that Joey was having a rough time, he didn't mean for me to leave and just give him some space to work through it.

No. It was time to leave the cynical behind and I knew it. Terry gave me a couple of valium and a half gram of coke for the long ride back to Boston.

How small Joey looked to me now. I'd spent three years building him up, traded my dreams for his and loved him to the best of my ability. This was the breaking point – Joey had sunk, in my view, lower to the ground than the chassis on any of his cars.

You know how you know when it's really time to leave? All at once, the person you are – who you really are at the core of your being – re-enters your body like a long lost soul. You feel the strength of who you are – your own character – and you know you wouldn't trade it for anything.

Your course may be uncharted, you may be leaving with just the clothes on your back, but the window is open and you know it's time to fly.

I spent two days back in Boston, half expecting Joey to call and apologize. He did not. I bought a one-way ticket home – to Baltimore. I packed two suitcases, my dog, and left a lovely picture of myself strategically placed so that Joey would see it as soon as walked in the apartment.

Why? At this point, I wanted him to feel small and remorseful for the things he'd said to me.

I loved him – for himself – warts and all. How dare he question my worth, love and value as a human being…

I was done.

Mom picked me up from the airport and was sorry to see me hurting so badly. In her usual way of wanting to make things better, she arranged for us to go to Ocean City, Maryland, for a few days. We shopped, talked and ate delicious seafood but nothing could fill the hole in my heart – not even the sound of the ocean waves crashing on the shore or the wide, expansive, endless ocean view from the balcony on the eighth floor of her friend's oceanfront condominium.

I still loved Joey very much and my leaving him, or wanting to leave him, was never a question of love. I was pretty sure I didn't want to marry him or have his children because of how he was reacting to the swiftly changing circumstances of our lives – but I had always loved him for who he was and what he had been for me.

Something was still yanking on my soul causing a deep yearning for something I couldn't name, in my heart. It was safe here at the beach because Joey didn't know how to reach me – if he did happen to try. Soon Mom and I would be going back to Baltimore and I felt the need to make a plan – any plan that would take me away and out into the world of self discovery and purpose. I called Scott before we left the beach, he was now living in LA, and told him about the break-up with Joey and that I was thinking of going West. Scott encouraged me to visit, soon.

I borrowed money from my mom for a one-way ticket to LA and flew out to California with $8 in my purse. I didn't care that I didn't have money or know anyone other than Scott – I had the freedom to dream my own dreams and hopefully discover what I could do well in this world.

As usual, Scott was happy to see me and eager to hear about the band. I was hurt, deeply hurt, and still very much in love with Joey. Scott wanted sex and just like when we had fooled around before, I was numb, only now I found myself coming face to face with mistakes I was making in my foolish attempt to protect my heart by going through the motions with Scott.

Scott worked days so I found myself walking the residential neighborhood streets shortly after I arrived. One morning I met a seemingly nice, long haired man walking his dog on a street near Scott's house – who seemed friendly, funny and harmless. He invited me into his house for tea and before I knew it he yanked a fully erect penis out of his pants and began to masturbate right there on his couch sitting across from me.

I didn't know what to think other than the West Coast was certainly very different from the East Coast. I wasn't scared; he wasn't threatening me, just clearly enjoying himself and from the look of it would be finished quickly. With an unusual sense of politeness I waited about two minutes and he was done. I thanked him for the tea and left.

As I walked back to Scott's house I wondered about his neighbor's behavior: was it indicative of a cultural difference between the two coasts or perhaps was I just an East Coast prude? Was it me? Was I attracting this lunacy? What started to creep into my thinking was the thought that somehow this experience must be my fault. Again, I felt sick and awful inside – just like I did after being raped a few years earlier.

During the three years I spent with Joey I never gave any thought to the rape after telling Joey about it. The experience wasn't gone; it had just been buried deep inside. Feelings were beginning to emerge from a deep emotional wound that I didn't consciously know I had.

With my awakening consciousness I knew I didn't want meaningless, robotic sex with Scott or anyone. I wanted love – real love – like the kind I had for Joey and that he did his best to give me. I was lost and desperately wanted to find myself – my path – the journey that would lead me to somehow making a difference and a contribution to this insanely spinning planet.

Nothing felt right. I spent hours, days, trying to figure it out. What was my calling? What was I put on this earth to do? Who was I – who the hell was I?

I had taken a huge first step in leaving Joey and another in flying to the West Coast. Now what?

It had been three weeks since I left Boston. I hadn't talked to Terry, Joey or anyone connected with the band. I walked up to Hollywood Boulevard, found a phone booth and called Terry in Boston. When Terry answered the phone and realized it was me there was suddenly deep concern and hesitation in her voice. I knew something was terribly wrong. She told me that Joey had fallen asleep at the wheel in the Ferrari on the Mass Pike and totaled his car. He had a head injury.

I hung up the phone without saying goodbye and called home – our home in Boston. Joey's dad answered the phone and again I heard the same deep concern and hesitation in his voice when he realized it was me. He passed the phone to his wife Doris and she, in her calm, task master way told me she didn't think it was a good idea for me to talk to Joey. I could hear Joey in the background yelling, "Is it her? Is it her? Is that Nancy?"

I could tell he snatched the phone quickly from his mom by the whooshing sound of air before he spoke – shouted – "You, you witch. You did this to me. You cursed me. You made this happen!!!"

Doris took the receiver from Joey and said, "I really don't think it's a good idea for you to ever call this house again." With that, she gently hung up the phone before I could utter another word.

I stood in the phone booth shaking and crying hysterically.

Was Joey okay? Would he be okay? How badly was he injured? I managed to call Terry back to find out. She told me the details of the accident and that yes, he would be okay. Terry also told me that Joey blamed me for the accident because of what I had said to him before leaving The Cenacle.

I never wished or wanted any harm to come to Joey. When I spoke those words to him at The Cenacle, "Joey – I hope it doesn't take you smacking up this car on the Mass Pike to teach you a thing or two about where your priorities lie," it came from a place of deep, unexplainable "knowing." It was the same kind of "knowing" or clairvoyance that my maternal grandmother had. I didn't plan to say those words to him, I wasn't looking into the future; I had a prophetic gift for him about where he was headed, spiritually. Now I know that's a bold statement to make, one that could easily get me kicked out of many camps, but it's true nonetheless.

I sensed the same finality in Terry's voice that I'd heard in Joey's mom's voice; it was over. My home with Joey was no longer my home. My heart broke wide open in that moment in broad daylight in that phone booth and I didn't give a rat's ass who might be witnessing my breakdown. I was now doubled over, heaving with heartbreak and complete severance of the love and belonging I had once known.

Thoughts rapidly raced through my mind: Joey's not dead, he's gonna be okay. I didn't cause this, his parents are with him, they'll see him through, they'll give him the love and care that he needs, my home is not my home anymore, it's really over. Okay, I wanted my freedom, now I've got it – what the hell am I gonna do with it?

Boston's out, Joey's out, what am I going to do? I've got great, fast hands – I could be a card dealer in Vegas and make money for school. I could join the Navy – travel, see the world and have them pay for my education.

All of a sudden... BAM... lights flashing... thoughts stopped... I could be a make-up artist and help bring out the inner beauty in people to match their outer physical beauty. Where the hell did that come from? I remembered Joey once telling me, "You've got a real knack for that make-up stuff, Nan. If you ever wanted to go into business with it, I'd back you."

Obviously I didn't want his money. Joey was more than frugal with his money so I knew he must have seen something in me that I didn't see in myself; a talent for doing something well. That was it. It was an epiphany in a California phone booth where just minutes before, my life as I knew it, had come to a screeching halt. I would become a make-up artist and I was in the perfect place to do it: Hollywood.

I opened the door to the phone booth and a black, mid-sized sedan pulled up alongside the curb next to me. The passenger window opened and a man asked, "Do you know of a good restaurant in this area?"

"No," I replied.

"Well, I'm looking for a nice place to have dinner – would you care to join me?"

Again, he seemed harmless enough. He was a well dressed Asian man, probably in his early thirties and I was hungry. I answered him by saying, "Well, how about I walk along the street while you drive and if we happen to find a nice restaurant in the next block, I'll have dinner with you."

He nodded, smiled and drove very slowly alongside the sidewalk. There was a nice restaurant in the next block, he parked and we went in and had a lovely dinner. I told him my story of how I had landed in LA and the earth shaking epiphany I had just experienced in the phone booth. He said he wanted to help me and that he needed a housekeeper. I gave him Scott's number and told him I'd think about it.

The next day I called the California Cosmetology Board to inquire about becoming a licensed make-up artist. I was told that I'd have to become a cosmetologist (hair dresser) in order to legally do make-up in the state of California because there wasn't a separate license for just doing make-up. Ridiculous. I didn't want to do hair, just make-up. Okay, I'll go to Florida, stay with my grandparents and get a license to do make-up there. But first I needed to raise the money for the airplane ticket and I had a tooth in my mouth that was beginning to shout for attention.

When the mysterious man who took me to dinner the night before called, I told him that I would clean his house because I needed money to get to Florida. I took several busses to get to his home and cleaned it top to bottom. He paid me well – more than I'd asked and drove me back to Scott's.

Scott was appalled that I would meet a man on the street, have dinner with him, clean his house and let him drive me home. He said the man and his car creeped him out. Scott was also not happy that I wasn't willing to have sex with him that night or any other night. He suggested I find another place to stay.

The Asian man was more than happy to let me stay in his guest room until I was financially able to go to Florida. I was twenty-one and dumb as a daisy. He had a small, black attaché case, maybe 8x10 inches, which he carried with him everywhere he went. He was always carrying it under his arm or left it to sit next to him in the car.

When I told him how badly my tooth hurt he made an appointment for me with a dentist in Beverly Hills. The tooth that hurt so badly was one that had had root canal started in but not completed before I left Boston. When the dentist popped off the temporary crown puss shot up everywhere like an intense volcanic eruption. The pain was gone immediately but the root canal needed to be finished after all the infection cleared. I scheduled an appointment for the following week and started antibiotics.

The Asian man drove me to the 3-hour appointment the following week and said he would be back to pick me up. Before I got out of the car I was looking at the small black case sitting next to him and

I was finally curious enough to ask what was in it and why did he always have it with him? He said it was something he needed for his job. I asked why he needed it today when he wasn't working and he said that he was always working. Okay, I give up, what's in the case? I didn't believe him when he told me it held a gun and that I should never touch it or ask any more questions about his work. I thought he was an actor, why would he need a gun? It puzzled me but then many things did in Hollyweird.

The dentist finished in just under three hours and said that one of his patients wanted to meet me. He said the man had been in to see him the previous week when I was there, saw me when I was leaving the office and asked that his next appointment be scheduled for right after mine. Okay, what does he want? The dentist said his patient just wanted to have coffee with me and that there was a lovely outdoor café next door. He told me not to worry; said he'd known him for years and that he was a very nice man. Recognizing that I might need a little more encouragement, he offered the fact that his patient lived next door to the movie actor, Ernest Borgnine. I loved the television series he'd starred in, "McHale's Navy."

I had a few minutes before the odd Asian man would be back to pick me up so after the dentist introduced us I agreed to have coffee with him. He charmingly told the office assistant that he needed to re-schedule his appointment because something wonderful had come up. Both smiling, with a hint of familiarity, we swooned next door for coffee and pastry. I thought I saw the Asian man drive by but knew it hadn't been three hours yet. This man, Jeffrey Konvitz, was an author, movie producer and a genuinely nice Jewish man originally from New York. We were enjoying our lively conversation and good coffee when the Asian man quietly appeared next to me and whispered in my ear that was time to go. The black case was now at my eye level.

Scared to death, I looked pleadingly at Jeff and said, "No, I'm not ready to leave." He pushed the case into my ribs and said, "We're leaving now."

"I'm not going anywhere with you," I said in a panic as Jeff asked him what was in the case? I told him a gun and Jeff called the waiter over who was watching the whole thing and told him to call the police. The Asian man left as quickly and quietly as he had appeared, long before the police arrived. The police took a full report and I told them all I wanted was my belongings back; they were still in his home. Jeff said I could stay at his house and he arranged for a police escort a few days later so that I could safely go in and get my things.

Son of a gun took my writing journals and had copied my phone book. I would later find out that he'd called my mother, Scott, Joey, Tom and Terry and told them all that I was strung out on drugs, prostituting myself and asked if they knew my whereabouts stating that he only wanted to help me.

I was grateful to Jeff for getting me out of that mess and opening his home to me. He called my mom to tell her I was okay, that I was staying with him for a few days and that she could rest easy; he would help me figure things out.

Jeff bought me a ticket to Miami, drove me to the airport, told me to stay out of trouble and have a great life. They don't come any nicer.

My grandparents were there, waiting inside at the airport to pick me up as they had my entire life, for some much needed unconditional love and support. For a brief moment I felt like I was home.

I called the Florida Cosmetology Board and I was told that their laws were the same as California; I'd have to become a licensed hair dresser in order to do make-up in the state of Florida. I'd left California so quickly after the incident with the Asian man that it didn't occur to me to stop, find the phone number and make a long distance call to the Florida State Board to check their governing laws for make-up artists. I assumed that only California could have such an absurd law.

My seventy year-old grandpa lovingly told me that he'd been to an Aerosmith concert and that he now had a 'good grasp' of that lifestyle and what goes on in that culture. God bless him, he loved me so much that he'd bought a ticket and went to a show to check things out firsthand. He encouraged me to pick up a trade, like becoming a make-up artist, do it with my whole heart and know that such skill I could take with me wherever I went. He suggested that I return to Baltimore and get started.

My friend Dick Cresci, whose grandpa had invented and patented the hydraulic lift on trucks and the hydraulic carrier tunnel that goes out from the airport terminal to the plane, told me that he would be taking the family yacht from Bal Harbor up to New Jersey in a couple of days and that he and the captain needed a cook onboard. Although being a galley wench onboard this 37 foot Chris Craft yacht wasn't a paid position, it was a free passage and I was too proud to ask anyone for money. I would make my own way to this new life and new possibility that was pulling me forward.

We spent ten glorious days cruising up the Intracoastal Waterway with perfect weather. Dolphins playfully swam next to the ship and swarms of white butterflies paused as we crossed their path. Frank Sinatra loudly crooned, 'Come Fly with Me,' in the background from high tech speakers above and below deck. The sun on the water warmed my soul in a way that I'll never forget.

We docked in Annapolis, Maryland promptly at noon on July 4th, 1977. Mom was there waiting, as promised, to pick me up. We drove to her house in Baltimore. As I was taking my luggage into her house I picked up the newspaper lying at her front door. I can't explain it, but I knew that something was waiting for me inside of that newspaper. There was. It was an ad for About Faces School of Make-up Artistry that promised you could apply for a state issued Maryland Make-up Artist license upon completion of the course. I registered for the course the next day.

My first teacher was Wilhelmina Beaumont, a well established Baltimore make-up artist, esthetician and a former Playboy Bunny in Baltimore. Willi was five years older than me and had been a Training Bunny in the Playboy Club. Training Bunnies were dispassionate drill sergeants during Playboy boot camp because it was up to them to make sure that their trainees would uphold the standards of Playboy and be able to handle themselves well in any situation inside the Club. I admired them.

Willi took me under her wing and with the same commitment and dedication that she'd had with Playboy, trained me in the art, skill and business of cosmetics. Willi was also responsible for the national sales of About Faces Cosmetics and eventually took the line to London for international distribution.

Willi was blonde, sexy, and Barbara Streisand beautiful. She was the most direct, professional go-getter independent woman I'd ever met. I was thrilled to have her mentor me. There was an opening in the About Faces Salon for an esthetician's apprentice and Willi recommended me for the job. The position paid $2 an hour and I'd be trained by some of the industry's finest in skincare, waxing and massage. I gratefully accepted the opportunity and loved the work from the first moment I stepped into the salon.

Gloria Brennan was the best of the best with make-up and her sister Terry could wax a gorilla in under an hour. Both were from South America. Mona Lindblom, hailing from Sweden, was unmatched in teaching how to give the world's best facial treatment. My specialized training program would be a yearlong with these incredible master teachers.

Shortly after I began working in the salon I heard that Aerosmith was coming to the Baltimore Civic Center and unresolved feelings about my relationship with Joey made their way to the surface. My mom suggested that I write him a letter and take it to him. I wasn't sure what I wanted to say; I loved him, yes, but I'd also found what I'd been looking for in terms of a career. Mom painstakingly composed a letter and I copied it over in my hand writing and took it down to the Civic Center when I knew the crew would be there setting up the equipment. I gave the letter to Kelly and he said he'd take it to Joey.

Joey called me at Mom's after reading the letter and asked me to come down to his hotel room. I remember walking into his room, scared, nervous and uncertain as to what my motivation was for being there. We hugged each other for a few minutes and then Joey sat in the one chair that was in the room and I sat on the edge of the bed. Joey was freshly showered and wearing jeans and a button down shirt. I was tanned and wearing white tennis shorts and a white

French t-shirt. I knew my motivation for choosing the clothes I wore; I wanted Joey to see that I was well, fit, able and had taken on a new life. What I remember most was that Joey just kept Mona Lisa smiling at me so intensely that any thoughts or words I may have had fled my mind. He seemed to have a tremendous sense of peace.

I rambled on about exercise, diet and nutrition. I could hardly look at him because every time I did, there was that warm, peaceful look of unconditional love on his face. Thoughts continued to race through my mind: What did I want? Why was I there? Did I really want to give up this new found sense of freedom, discovery and wonder of what the world was like outside of Aerosmith? Not a chance. I now had evidence that there was a bigger world waiting to be explored and I would light my own path through it.

But Joey's familiar smile made me want to get up and squeeze in the chair with him. The Mona Lisa smile was the one that would break across his face just before he would tell me how beautiful it was to watch me cross the threshold and blossom into womanhood during the time we were together. I wanted to cry with him, forgive him and myself and bury my head in his chest.

Dear God, why couldn't I just move five feet from the bed and tell the man how much I loved him?

Why couldn't he get up from the chair and say, "Nan, I love you. Please come home."

In the deafening silence I could hear the high pitched sound of the air conditioning unit in his room blasting and feel the cold air on my exposed skin. Damn it. Why couldn't I expose my feelings?

Afraid that one of us would get up and move toward the other and I would become lost again in his world without dreams of my own, I stood up and said something that my mom had said in the letter.

"Joey, I need money."

Joey stood up and asked, "Why should I give you money?"

Reciting more from the letter, I told him, "Because I spent three years with you helping you to advance your career and you made me accustomed to a certain type of lifestyle."

I hated myself in that moment for blurting out those words that were not my own. I loved him when he was poor, I loved him in that moment and the fucking money was the demise of our dreams.

What the hell was I doing? This wasn't me or the words in my heart.

Joey lit a Marlboro Red cigarette and asked if I had anything else to say.

I looked closer into that open and honest face that I had loved so dearly and remembered what it was like to live dreamless in the shadow of his spotlight, and said "No, that's it. I don't have anything else to say."

When I got back to Mom's she asked me how it went and if we were back together – did I ask him for a second chance? I told her that I did not and that it was one of the hardest things I'd ever done. She asked if I had asked him for money and I burst into shameful tears. I told her that I didn't feel that Joey owed me anything other than maybe an apology for the way he behaved and the things he had said to me when I left The Cenacle.

Fate might find us again but in the meantime I needed a second job to support the in-salon education and buy a car. So I picked up a second job waitressing in a busy Italian Restaurant. The first night on the job, the owner asked me who I was and would I like to go out with him? Although he was a dreamy, dark haired Italian man, I told him no because I didn't think it was a good idea to date the boss. He said, "You're fired. What time can I pick you up Saturday night?'

Umberto owned a couple of Italian restaurants, a motel and a large night club with live entertainment. Mostly he booked regional bands that would be the house band for a week or two and occasionally big acts that appealed to older Italians. He was ten years older than me and I spent almost two years with him. I had the same trouble with him that I'd had with Joey; I didn't want to marry him or have his children, but I didn't want to let him go either.

For almost a year between 1978 and 1979, I lived between Umberto's house and an apartment that I shared with Willi. There was a nightclub in Baltimore called Girard's, said to have been built by the same people who built Studio 54 in New York. People would travel from Washington, DC and Northern Virginia on weeknights to wait in line to get into the club. Willi would often call me to ask if my "jailor" would let me out so we could go and get down at Girard's. Willi was a lot of fun in those days.

On Halloween, 1978, Willi insisted that we go to the Halloween Party at Girard's. Umberto forbade me, which really pissed fun, loving, independent Willi off and she knew I really wanted to go. She told me not to worry, she'd take care of our costumes and Umberto would never know we were there. Willi rented a two person bull's costume, bought matching black tights and sneakers for us to wear underneath. She would be the head and I the tail. We laughed hysterically as we practiced walking like a dancing bull in the apartment before we went out. I had a nagging feeling that Umberto would be at Girard's to check up on me and if I was being obedient to him. Willi assured me that even if he did show up he'd never be able to guess that it was us inside the costume.

We danced our way into Girard's, no one knowing who the playful bull was. My legs were the bull's back legs and her legs were the bull's front legs. I held her waist underneath the costume so that we'd move together as one bull unit. About an hour later I noticed two feet standing next to me wearing Italian leather shoes. I'd know those feet anywhere; it was Umberto. The music was so loud I had a really hard time telling Willi that Umberto was standing next to us. I kept pushing her to move forward, go in another direction and she was quite happy to be standing where we were. Finally, I pinched her butt and then head butted her towards the ladies room. When we got into the ladies room I was able to tell her that Umberto was there.

"So what," was Willi's response, "He doesn't know it's us. Relax. You can't let a man lead you around forever. Let's go have a good time."

And a good time we had. Willi made sure we danced next to Umberto, even rubbing her bull's head on his back. I was scared and laughing so hard that I nearly wet my pants.

Willi had been telling me about an outrageous hair dresser that she wanted me to meet who lived and worked in affluent Montgomery County, Maryland. She said his name was Richard; he had long wavy purple hair and wore high top red tennis shoes. Willi said that he and I were a perfect match and even if I didn't want to go out with him, just meet him. Sound familiar? One night while sleeping at Umberto's, I woke us both up speaking Richard's name out loud in my sleep. Umberto wanted to know who the hell Richard was. I told him I didn't know, which I didn't, because we hadn't yet met.

On a Wednesday afternoon, March 14th, 1979, I called Willi in her office and told her that we had to go to Girard's that night. Something big was going to happen. I didn't know what, I only knew that I had a date with destiny and needed to show up. Willi trusted my intuition and we both were full of expectancy and anticipation. Just before leaving for Girard's my Yorkie, Nathan, slipped out of the house and ran into the woods. I didn't think I'd ever get him back again and was ready to cancel going to Girard's when Nathan pranced up next to me ready to go back inside. He'd never run off before.

Once inside Girard's, Willi and I stood at the front bar near the street entrance to the club. I kept watching the front door, knowing that something incredible was about to happen. Two eyes locked into mine as they rounded the corner into the club. I could feel Willi pulling on my arm and saying something but I couldn't hear her or the music, I could only see the eyes coming toward me. It was like two polarized planets on course to collide within minutes.

Face to face with the eyes, all seven chakras ringing and connecting with the human body in front of me, sound returned. "Nancy this is Richard. Richard, the one I've been telling you about. Richard, this is my friend Nancy." I could hear Willi's words but she sounded like she was a world, a dimension apart from us.

Richard said, "Let's dance."

He took my hand and we glided to the dance floor like we'd done this a thousand times before. We danced two or three songs, eyes never parting, communicating lifetimes of love without speaking a word. When the music stopped, we finally blinked, smiled and parted, navigating our separated orbits off the dance floor without saying a word.

I walked over to Willi, standing at the middle of the room bar now, next to the dance floor. She was thrilled that Richard and I had finally met. I still had no words, only a deep sense of satisfaction of having been seen, known and loved by a kindred spirit. It was the afterglow of lovemaking outside of a physical plane. This is the best I can describe this transcendental experience with another human being.

Willi pointed to Richard who was now sitting on the couches near the dance floor and said that I should go talk to him. I walked over to where he was sitting and found him asleep. I sat on his lap, he opened his eyes and said, "Oh it's you. Hello. Are you going to the New York Hair Show this weekend?"

"Yes", I replied.

"Where are you staying?", he asked softly.

I gave him the name of my hotel and he told me that he would see me in New York.

Now remember, these events occurred at a time when there were no cell phones, computers or GPS systems. Luck, happenstance, destiny or sheer determination is how people found each other.

I drove to New York and when I entered my hotel room, there were a dozen red roses from Umberto waiting for me. I wondered if I'd see Richard at the Hair Show but I certainly wasn't about to go looking for him. I was there to gather information for About Faces and bring it back.

At the end of the first day when I returned to my hotel there were two messages waiting for me; one from Umberto and the other from Richard. I called Umberto first and thanked him for the beautiful roses. Next, I called Richard and he invited me to the Paul Mitchell Artistic Design Team party. I told him that I was really too tired, having left Baltimore before the sun came up to drive to New York and that all I really wanted was room service and a good night's sleep. Richard said that this party was by invitation only and that I could possibly make some great connections for my boss. He asked that I

139

would not rule it out; rest, get something to eat and he would call me back in an hour.

I was almost asleep when Richard called again. I'd eaten a big meal and left a hot fudge sundae sitting on the tray beside me. Richard said he was on his way to pick me up, get ready, he'd see me in fifteen minutes. Without further discussion, I put the ice-cream sundae outside on the window sill in the cold air so I could have it later and got dressed.

Richard knocked on my door promptly fifteen minutes later and I let him in for minute while I put on lipstick. He asked about the roses and if I had a boyfriend. I told him that I did and we left for the hotel where the party was being held. Just before we reached the room, Richard stopped me in the hotel hallway and playfully and deliberately planted a hard kiss on my mouth biting my lower lip, causing it to bleed.

I wasn't sure if I liked being kissed that way or if I'd ever let him kiss me again. We stayed only a short time at the party and Richard walked me back to my hotel. We were almost there when he said he was starving and asked if I had anything to eat. I remembered the ice-cream sundae sitting outside the window sill. I told him I'd share it with him but he'd have to leave after that. We ate the sundae slowly, sharing one spoon. After licking all the ice-cream off the last bite Richard asked if he could please stay the night. He was exhausted as well and promised that he wouldn't touch me.

Too tired to argue and fairly certain that he'd behave, I let him. We slept well together. When morning came he asked, like the cutest little boy I'd ever heard, "Could we make love?"

With Richard, I had no desire to make him wait three weeks as I had Joey. I was certain that we were about to spin out of this world and into a beautiful new Milky Way.

For the remainder of the day we were inseparable, attending every possible class and visiting all the booths at the Hair Show.

I was scheduled to fly from Baltimore to Miami the next day for vacation, so I needed to drive back to Baltimore to catch my flight. Richard persuaded me to stay an extra day, fly out of New York instead and let him and Willi drive my car home. This way we'd have twelve more hours to explore each other's minds, bodies and souls. I got onboard with the mission. I was lost in love and lust with my feet barely touching the ground.

In Miami, I had another dozen red roses from Umberto waiting for me at my grandparent's house. I had to tell him – but what did I have to tell him? That I'd been unfaithful, that it was over, that I'd met someone else? Once again I figured I'd use the time at the beach to sort things out. The truth was I didn't want to be with Umberto forever like he wanted to be with me and it was unfair of me to stay with him knowing that. I called him and told him so. He asked that I give it time, think things over and we'd talk when I got back.

Richard could hardly wait for me to get back and his enthusiasm was contagious. I started to get really excited about seeing him again and terrified at the same time. A case of measles kept me in Miami a few days longer than planned and while Richard's anticipation of seeing me grew, I was content to wait a little longer before flying home.

Richard wanted to pick me up at the airport so I changed my flight to fly into Washington National because it was closer for him than Baltimore. He was so excited to see me that he went to the wrong airport. He went to Baltimore and I landed in Washington. No cell phones. After waiting over an hour for each other in different airports, we both somehow knew to show up at Girard's and there we would find each other again. This time it was my turn to come around the corner inside of Girard's and see his eyes peeled on the front door waiting for mine.

Again, the earth shifted on its axis when we saw each other. Richard asked where my luggage was and when I told him it was in the coat room he said, "Good. Let's get it. You're coming home with me and I'm never letting you go."

What am I getting myself into now and do I care? Negative. Let's launch this craft.

We got to his house in warp speed and went straight to bed, a water bed. After beautiful love making, he would not let me go –

141

some part of his body was always touching mine. Even when I tried to inch over to the outside of the bed to look at the moonlight shining through the window, he pulled me back into his arms. I tried but couldn't look away as I had learned to do with Joey to protect my heart.

As I lay there that first night with him I tried to figure out why this handsome, aware and talented human being was choosing me. Richard had young John Travolta good looks and was the most gorgeous man I'd ever seen. He was smart, funny and caring. I didn't know why, but something deep inside whispered to me to let go and trust the process. I said goodbye to Umberto and hello to my new future.

Days turned into weeks, weeks turned into months of bliss with Richard. I told my mother and Willi that if he asked me to marry him I would say yes in a heartbeat. I'd met most of Richard's friends and they shared many of the same qualities as Richard; they were clearly living in the now, had bold ass dreams and communicated with a transparency and honesty like I'd never seen. They were genuinely happy people and authentically interested in others. It was as if they lived their lives looking for what was possible rather than self-limiting beliefs about what couldn't be. Richard and most of his friends had done the EST Training.

While dusting the furniture in our living room one morning I picked up a stack of dusty magazines to organize and found a small, thin brown paper notebook. It had the EST logo on the front and scribbled words, 'private and confidential.' Okay, whose was it? For a nano second I thought about not opening it and putting it back on the pile.

No way. Curiosity got the best of me and I opened it and read the words, "Be able to tell a girl I love her. " Next page, "Tell just one girl that I love her." Next page, boldly spelled out in capital letters, "TELL A GIRL I LOVE HER!"

Who wouldn't want to be that girl?

This was Richard's EST seminar notebook. I closed it, put it back on the stack and cleaned the rest of the living room as if the Pope were coming. Then I called the EST Training office and registered for the next course. Richard came home and said we'd been invited to go swimming at a friend's pool. I was so damn happy I did five flips off the diving board. I'd never done a flip in my life.

A few nights later, on a Friday night, Richard called to tell me he was going out after work with some of the crew from work and that he shouldn't be out too late. He got home very late, stinking drunk and had five or six other inebriated people with him. One sloshed and slutty looking teeny bopper was hanging on to him trying to hold her drunk self up. She kept telling him she loved him. Then he kissed her.

Exit, stage left; I'm not going down this road again. Richard and the young lady stumbled into the living room and passed out on the couch. I went to bed.

The next morning I went to work having determined in my heart that it was over with Richard. He called to apologize and I told him I was done; I was closing the book on our relationship. I'd been down this road before and wasn't going back again. He asked me if I would just close this one chapter. I told him I'd think about it and I made plans to have another hair dresser who really wanted to go out with me pick me up at Richard's after work.

Physically and emotionally leaving the relationship was an old and well established survival mechanism by this time and the only one I knew to reach for to protect my heart from further injury.

My date was prompt to pick me up at Richard's and we were all surprised that they knew each other. Richard asked when I would be back and I smart-assedly replied, "I shouldn't be too late."

Well, I got drunk, good and drunk and my date took me to his apartment and put me to bed.

When he drove me home the next morning I was hung over and wanted nothing but a long hot bubble bath and a couple of aspirin. Richard came into the bathroom while I was soaking and asked me how was my date, did I have a good time, and lastly, did I sleep with him.

"It was okay. I got drunk and no, I didn't sleep with him!" I was angry, with my head-pounding self and amazed by how calm Richard seemed asking me these questions. I then added in my date's defense, "He didn't even try to touch me!"

"Of course he didn't. He didn't try anything because he knows that by not trying he'll get more from you later."

Where on earth did this calm sage find this wisdom I wondered, listening to Richard's words as he continued.

"I'll bet he even offered to bring you home." I couldn't wait to get to the EST Training; I wanted to be as smart and confident as Richard was.

He had more to say, "Well, I've decided that I'm going to do one of three things: I'm going to find a psychiatrist, go to AA, or ask you to marry me."

Holy crap. What kind of proposal was that? Wait, did he just propose?

"Nancy, will you marry me?" Richard still had the same calm, certain demeanor.

Well, shit. "Yes. But you better be certain that this is what you really want and that you're ready for it."

"I am." With that he left the bathroom and I submerged myself under the bubbles. Holy crap, I'm getting married!

Richard returned with phone in hand and said, "Here. My mom wants to welcome you to the family."

"Nancy, congratulations and welcome to the family. I look forward to meeting you. Richard asked me for my mother's ring which my daughter Penny has. We'll make sure we get it to him. Welcome. I'm so happy for you both. Richard told me he proposed while you were in the bathtub so I won't keep you, again, congratulations and welcome." Dang, the man is making it seriously real.

Richard asked me if we could have an engagement party, cook outside on the grill and invite all our friends to come over. He said he wanted to share the news of our engagement and this special day with everyone we knew. About sixty people showed up to congratulate us.

I was still reeling with bride-to-be excitement when later that week we were invited to yet another neighbor's house for a swim and a game of water volleyball. It was so much fun until the ball was hit out of the pool and I jumped out to chase it. It was nighttime and I didn't see that a drain was missing its cover. As I ran for the ball, my foot and lower leg went straight down into the open drain hole, breaking a bone in my foot and tearing the crap out of my shin. It was excruciatingly painful and I, not realizing how badly I was hurt, thought I could tough it out until morning. When we woke up, I realized I couldn't put any weight on it. Richard took me to an ER. I remember how concerned he was, telling me that he was going to find out if he could add me to his health insurance policy before we were married and that he would get the ring from his sister that week. Everything would be okay.

With a fractured bone in my foot and a shredded ligament over my shinbone, I'd be on crutches and in a hard cast for at least four weeks. Richard told me not to worry; he'd take care of the house, the bills and me.

Three days later, Richard came home and told me that he was going to start playing the drums again a few nights a week with a band in Georgetown. The next night would be the first night he'd be performing with a band that'd just lost their drummer. I didn't know he played the drums. Fear ran through me when he told me. He wasn't going to take care of me, he was going to leave... Or this was how his 'playing the drums' occurred for me. I'd been down this road before...

The similarities were starring me right in the face: he was five years older than me, a Jewish drummer, and would now be playing music in front of a lot of hot looking, out to meet the boys in the band, women and girls. I couldn't see how this would have a happy ending.

At twenty-three, I didn't yet have a wise woman's understanding heart; I had the heart of a scared little girl who was telling me to leave him first, before he had an opportunity to leave me. My heart's protection mechanism kicked into high gear, survival instinct took

145

over and I called the man who'd come to my rescue twice before, Dick Cresci.

Dick had helped to soothe my heart when Joey went to Hawaii without me and we got lost under the Miami moon in 1976. He came to my rescue again after I left Joey in 1977 and needed a passage from Miami to Baltimore. I felt that I needed him now to white knight me out of this seemingly similar situation with Richard.

I was able to reach him in New Jersey. Dick – calm, sympathetic and curious about my predicament, asked me a few key questions about Richard:

"Does he drink?" – Yes.

"Does he do drugs?" – Yes.

"Has he cheated on you?" – Almost.

"What does he do for a living?" – He's a hairdresser and a drummer.

"Sweetheart, I'm sending a plane. Pack a bag and get to the airport."

I realize now that I was on auto pilot with a mission to flee in order to avoid possible future pain, but all I knew at that time was that I had to get out, even if it was at a slow hobble on crutches.

I knew that my sudden and abrupt departure without explanation would hurt Richard deeply and that he would intuitively know that there was more to it than just wanting to visit a friend. I couldn't explain my actions to myself, let alone anyone else as I didn't understand them, at the time.

I remembered leaving Joey at The Cenacle and the pain that followed after I told him that I needed to get away.

Richard got home from work early, twenty minutes before the taxi was scheduled to pick me up. He was talking fast and telling me how excited he was to finally be playing drums again and that he needed a quick shower before leaving for the gig in Georgetown. Would I please lay out his show clothes while he jumped in the shower and find his red sneakers? I did as he asked.

The cab pulled up in the driveway while Richard was in the shower. I motioned to the driver that I'd be right out. Richard raced from the shower, quickly put on the clothes I'd laid on the bed and grabbed his sneakers.

"Richard," I began, I'm leaving for a few days. I'm going to see an old friend and I'll be back Sunday or Monday."

Richard, now sitting on the bed and bent over tying the laces on his red sneakers spotted my suitcase next to me on the floor by the bedroom door. He looked up at me and realized that I was already packed and ready to go. A look of sheer fear and abandonment came over his face as he asked me where I was going and when I would be leaving.

"I'm leaving now. There's a cab outside waiting to take me to the airport."

His face went pale and his hands trembled as he fumbled to tie his shoe laces. Afraid that I might see this beautiful spirit of a man cry, I grabbed my bag and headed out the front door.

I knew how deeply I had hurt Richard and that leaving was probably a mistake but survival instinct was fully operational and I got in the cab. I cried all the way to the airport.

Dick was there to meet me when the plane landed and I told him that I thought I'd made a huge mistake and that I should probably just turn around and go back. Dick shushed my tears and told me not to worry; we'd figure this out.

We talked, went to dinner and then on to the casinos in Atlantic City. We were on a winning streak, already having won a thousand dollars but I couldn't wait to get back to Dick's house to call Richard.

It was late when I called him and told him how sorry I was to have left so abruptly. I was glad to find him home alone and not drunk or high after the gig in Georgetown. I gave him Dick's number and said I'd be home in a couple of days.

Richard called me the next day and said that he had been offered a free plane ticket to the West Coast with a friend who had a business meeting in LA. He said he would be back in a couple of days. He said he'd never been to California and he really wanted to see it. And, after all, this was a free trip. I told him that you can't see LA in a couple of days, it would take weeks.

He was gone when I got home. He called three days later and said that I was right; you can't see LA in a couple of days. He was going to stay a while longer. And he added, "When I get back we're getting married. I don't care if it's on top of a mountain or the backyard. Call my sister, call the Rabbi and get things set up."

I knew in my heart of hearts that he was gone. The words meant nothing to me. I made no plans, I made no calls. Richard called three weeks later and said he'd be home the next day. I was in the middle of the two-weekend EST Training and in the bathtub when he came into the house. He walked into the bathroom and said,

"I'm moving to LA and I'm going solo. You're welcome to come as my make-up artist." It was harsh, very harsh.

He began selling everything in the house because he was starting over and wouldn't need all the things he'd accumulated. I completed the EST Training, crying all the way through it. Richard and seven of his friends showed up for my EST Graduation and I had one thing to say to each one of them as I left the hotel ballroom, "Fuck you." I said it plainly and clearly seven times. Someone had left early missing the first, fully self-expressed and clearly communicated expression of my transformational experience with EST, "Fuck you too," I thought.

Richard was gone within a week with the love and support of all his friends. I moved back to my mom's and cried a river over having lost two men to LA.

My job at the salon was going great. I had a large following of wonderful clients and was making lots of money. I wanted to replace a front tooth crown that my dentist in Boston told me that he would love to do for me one day. He was also Steven Tyler's dentist. Willi and I drove to Boston after a cosmetic show in Philadelphia and stayed in the hotel with the roof top lounge where I had once worked. I wasn't looking forward to the process of replacing the crown because it meant the dentist had to pull the old one off in order to make a new one. Just after he pulled the crown off leaving me with only a stub of a front tooth, he left the room and said he'd be right back. When he returned he told me that Steven was there and would really love to come back and say hello. No, please no. I was having enough trouble being toothless all by myself. He patted me on the shoulder and said he understood and would give Steven my best.

Being back in Boston, I couldn't help but think of all the time I spent there, with and without Joey. Hearing the strong Bostonian accent I was reminded of Terry, Tom's wife, and how close we once had been. I hadn't talked to her since that day in the phone booth in LA. Willi encouraged me to call her. The number had changed so I called her mom, told her who I was, and got the new number. Terry was not happy to hear from me and not happy that her mom had given me the number. She said the Asian man had called her looking for me and told her the same outrageous story he'd told my mom. Unfortunately, she believed him and said she had nothing to say to me, please don't call again.

Crushed and toothless, thank God Willi was there to pick my heart up off the floor. I could have called Terry before then but I never thought she'd doubt me or close her heart to me.

I had to keep moving on, putting the past in the past. I began to assist, volunteer at EST events in Baltimore and Washington, DC. I didn't know exactly what I'd gotten out of the course but I enjoyed being around people who had completed the program. They were always up to something – trying to make the world a better place and they were so damn happy.

In 1980, I met Jerry Bridge at an EST Guest Event. He, like me, was assisting within the EST network. He was the happiest, most alive and uninhibited person I'd ever met. He had movie star good looks, a boisterous and clear voice, and a deeply compassionate nature. As I got to know him through assisting together at EST events I discovered that he genuinely loved people and always saw the best in them. Jerry saw what most people didn't; the inherent good in all human beings. If you told Jerry that you couldn't do something or that something was not possible, he would smile and say, why not?

He saw a world where anything was possible and nothing too far out of reach; a world that works for everyone. Death by hunger could be ended in our lifetime, wars could be stopped before they started, and hate could be eradicated from the face of the earth. Jerry believed that people were capable of going well beyond self-limiting ideas and self-imposed obstacles to discover and embrace their own greatness; that at the heart of the matter we're all the same and capable of being magnificent in each and every moment. Deep in the heart of all of us lives an extraordinary human being.

Jerry also believed that joy was our natural state of existence and if we weren't experiencing joy in the here and now – we could shift our perception of our circumstances and create joy. Happiness and love were a place to come from; not try to get to as a destination. Anything could be healed: people, relationships and even the planet.

For a long time I wondered if I had missed the Kool-aid table. Jerry was like the men and women who led the EST Training; he authentically believed these things to be so. And, he had a powerful way of communicating the possibility of a world such as this so that you wanted to board the next let's make a difference train.

Breakdowns are an opportunity for breakthroughs.

Happiness is a function of accepting what is.

In life you wind up with one of two things – the results you intended to produce, or the reasons why you failed to produce the intended results.

In Werner Erhard's words, "Love is granting another person the freedom to be the way they are and the way they are not."

It is possible to create a world that works for everyone.

Jerry believed, like EST founder, Werner Erhard, that "things could be created by your consideration alone; that we were all given a magic wand with which to create." Jerry believed that we are always the cause in the matter of our lives and responsible for how we experience our lives in each and every moment. We always have a choice as to how we experience ourselves and the world around us. There were many things that I didn't understand about the principles and distinctions of the EST Training but Jerry had it down pat and loved talking about it as much as he enjoyed living life and being in life this way, with these core beliefs.

Jerry and Werner Erhard both spoke of the attributes of being of "service" to other human beings; unselfishly giving of your time, talents and abilities to make a difference in the quality of someone else's life. Was it possible for someone not to have something to contribute? No. Everything could be offered up and given away as a gift: even your pettiness, anger and points of view. These altruistic virtues were very much like those of Mother Theresa, Gandhi and Nelson Mandela, who were often quoted in EST seminars.

"At all times and under all circumstances we have the power to transform the quality of our lives," said Werner Erhard.

On many levels I understood all of this but I had no magic wand, just a wish in my heart that I'd had since childhood. My maternal grandmother, with whom I lived until I was eight, would often point out the first star in the evening sky and tell me to make a wish. My wish was always the same: that people would love each other, that there would be no wars and that everyone would have enough to eat.

Wanting more, like the sun and the moon too, I volunteered to assist at the EST 6-Day Course in the mountains in upstate New York. The course was said to be arduously hard-core and required two months of training prior to going for the forty people selected to assist in its production. Jerry Bridge and his two friends, Cindy Rogers and Layne Humphrey, and I were amongst the small group from Baltimore chosen to go to the East Coast site, just north of Poughkeepsie, New York. It was a ten day assisting agreement. EST staff would be there to set up the ropes courses, manage the course content, and the well-being of the trainers while we prepared the grounds, cabins and Pritikin kitchen for the participants.

The ropes courses consisted of a Tyrolean traverse, mountainside rappel and a zip line. Each day would start with yoga just before sunrise followed by a one mile run up the mountain, no walking was permitted.

Participants would be coming into the course with all of their fears, concerns and desired outcomes for breakthroughs. It was made clear to us that we would, at times, literally have people's lives in our hands. For this reason, we needed to operate in a state of impeccable integrity, being our word at all times. I didn't know exactly what I was getting myself into; only that it was the Big Kahuna of the EST training.

There was a long list of what we could and could not bring including over the counter drugs, illegal drugs, alcohol and tobacco.

I'd been without nicotine for four days and was assigned to assist on the mountain top at the Tyrolean traverse line, harnessing and buckling the participants into safety gear with locking carabiners. When I was finished they would be double-checked by one more person and then hooked to the hundred foot line by the waist. The line extended from the top of one mountain to the top of another. In the middle was air; a deep ravine lay below. The participants had to cross the distance in between the two mountain tops, pulling themselves arm over arm while being suspended hundreds of feet in the air to reach the other side.

I was tired, hungry, dirty and woodsy bugs kept flying into my mouth. *Why was I here? What was I hoping to get out of this? Why the hell did I sign up for this? Oh, he's cute. Well, there are cute men here. She's wearing make-up; I can't believe she's wearing make-up out here in the woods! There must be an easier way to make a difference in the world than this.*

I was busy judging and evaluating everything within sight.

Right about that time I saw Hal Isen, a tall, mean looking, fierce faced EST trainer casually running up the mountain path toward me and the people I was locking into their gear. He glanced at my nametag and then looked up and through my little eyeballs. I looked back at him with the same fierce expression I'd perceived him to be giving me. His eyes grew wider as he shouted words at me piercing through and penetrating my internal dialogue like a swift Samurai's sword.

"Nancy, get out of your fucking head!"

What the fuck? Who the hell do you think you are, barking at me like that? I'm not getting paid for this aggravation buddy. You can go fuck...

I stopped mid-thought and burst out laughing.

Holy fucking shit...that was it!

The big "it" of EST – the transformational moment when one discerns the ramblings of one's own mind from one's true "being."

The judgments, evaluations, and wheels in my mind stopped.

Nothing was there: no thought, no worry or concern, nothing.

It was in that moment that a transformation occurred in me as I realized I was in my head and believing everything that little voice up there (in my mind) told me to be true. "It" was creating the reality of the world in which I was living.

I wasn't having thoughts; they were having me – for breakfast, lunch and dinner!

Nothing was there in that moment but me and another human being. No judgments, no evaluations: just me and the human being in front of me whom I was there to serve. Yee-hah, I got it. I got the EST Training, the transformational moment, the freedom and opportunity to just be – right then, right there in that moment on that mountain top. Hal-le-fucking-lujah! No disrespect to God intended.

The next participant to be safely harnessed was a small Asian man without arms. Looking into his eyes I saw a fully capable and well able human being – just like myself. He traversed the mountain tops hanging upside down using his feet to propel his body across the ravine.

The Zen koan (parable) for the assistants in the 6-Day Course was, "When I don't know who I am, I serve you. When I know who I am, I am you." This riddle is a powerful way to describe the ground of being of service to others. It is a beautiful way, or context, from which to look at the people who inhabit this world and how we choose to interact with them.

Jerry, my fellow 6-Day assistant, became my new best friend and partner in transformation. We went everywhere together in the transformational world of EST: the Graduate Seminars in Baltimore and Washington, special events with founder Werner Erhard in New York and Philadelphia, The Holiday Project, The Hunger Project and World Runners.

Jerry, twenty-two years old and two years younger than me, understood how badly my heart had been recently broken by

Richard's sudden departure to LA and was content to just hang out and be my friend. We shared a love for music and dancing and went out dancing, often.

Jerry and I even put a small rock band together with him playing drums and me attempting to be a lead female singer. We called it "Pretty Poison." I was more interested in designing a great album cover for the band than learning how to sing, so I borrowed Kyf Brewer's (lead singer for Baltimore's best band of the eighties, "The Ravyns") six and a half foot boa constrictor snake and hired a photographer to shoot the cover. We got epic pictures of me and a snake but the band broke up after a week.

In October of 1979, Richard and I were both scheduled to present at a Paul Mitchell Show in Maryland. I was glad to know ahead of time that I would be seeing him so that I could prepare for it. I expected to be quite emotional but confident in my own element of expertise, doing make-up and speaking on stage.

And, I'd just had mind blowing Trojan style Get Out of Your Fucking Head "6-Day" style sex with Kyf, outside on his bedroom balcony railing during a crack-the-sky light-up-the-world thunderstorm. So let Richard bring on his snake charming wistfulness; I would be the one standing firmly against his seductions.

Like a fly on honey, after the show he sought me out at the evening soiree and asked me to dance.

Why the hell didn't I leave? I didn't need to schmooze with artists and cosmetic manufacturers or advance my career. I wanted to see Richard and test the transformational waters. I expected I would be bold, beautiful and desirable. I was, and so was he. We swam in the bliss, again.

"Come to LA."

"As your make-up artist?"

"No, come because you want to and because you want to be with me."

"No. You can't be trusted."

"Yes I can."

"You're a lying sack of shit."

"Not all the time. I can be true. I love you and I love being with you. Come to LA."

"No, fuck no."

Bye-bye Richard, it felt great; absolutely great. I might occasionally miss what we never had, but in time I'd get over that too.

Jerry and I were married in a medieval castle during an ice storm on a Sunday, January 31st, 1981. He was also a Jewish drummer.

MOTHER NATURE'S SON – The Best Job on the Planet!

It was a fairytale wedding with a smorgasbord of Jewish drummers in the house at the castle. Jerry, his dad Melvin, and all three of Melvin's brothers played the drums and sang at our wedding.

I know, enough with the Jewish drummers already.

Like former CNN nighttime host, Larry King dated and married numerous birds of a feather, namely Playboy Bunnies, for me it was Jewish drummers. I dated four Jewish drummers and married one of them. I didn't deliberately go looking for them or ask for this card to be dealt to me, but I certainly attracted them into my broken soul with what they had to offer. They provided me a true sense of belonging to a well-meshed deeply passionate clan who had survived hell throughout history and treated me like a special little shiksa goddess.

Deeply wounded in childhood by teenage parents, sixteen and eighteen at the time of my birth, who didn't have a clue how to be married adults and raise children, my parents struggled and did the best they could. Not being able to trust my parents to provide and protect me, and meet basic human needs, too often I had to fend for myself. The exception was the six years my mom, brother and I lived with my grandparents in Miami Beach, Florida.

My parents divorced at eighteen and twenty and remarried each other at twenty four and twenty six.

As with all human beings, much of what I experienced in those young formative years shaped my view of the world, others and myself. There were predominant themes, patterns, and ways of being and behaviors that became neurologically grooved into my brain. No human being escapes this natural, evolutionary process of growth and development.

For me, many of the early experiences were extreme and traumatic. For all of us, there are definitely key moments, incidents, which will define who we are and how we will behave in the world. Most of this happens without us being aware of the decisions that we make at the time of the occurrence.

I'm not a doctor or a therapist; simply an aware human being who has taken on being the best damn human being I can be.

Jerry and I were well yoked. We both wanted to save the world and we were best friends.

One of the notions of EST was the notion of "being complete." If you are complete with something or someone, you are whole, complete and satisfied with that thing or that someone, without hesitation. Or, said another way, the Hebrew word "shalom" which translates to "nothing broken, nothing missing."

My brilliant and beautiful husband Jerry boldly asserted that I was not "complete" in my relationship with Joey. When I gave up being defensive about the idea of being "incomplete" with Joey Kramer, I realized that Jerry was right. Things were left in a mess when I left Joey washing his car at The Cenacle. He blamed me for the accident. When I saw him for twenty minutes in Baltimore a few months later we spoke of nothing relevant and I certainly had not revealed to him the truest words of my heart. I'd taken his matching family Moses necklace (Joey, Annabelle, Amy, Suzy and I were all given matching necklaces from Doris Kramer) and Ten Commandments charm that his mom gave him. I had his favorite black and gold scarf (the one on the cover of the "Get Your Wings" album) and the two silk cases for his Samurai swords from Japan. These things may seem trivial but when you're doing your best to live in a space of impeccable integrity in your life even the little things count.

Jerry also suggested that I needed to acknowledge Joey for the difference he made in my life including having seen a talent in me that I didn't see in myself which led to a very rewarding career.

Aerosmith was scheduled to perform at the Baltimore Civic Center on February 16, 1983. I decided that this would be the perfect opportunity to complete the past with Joey. Jerry and I would host an after party for the band at Girard's. I asked my friend, Layne Humphrey, who had stood for me when I got married to stand for me now and the success of the event. Success meant Joey showing up to the party and he and I having the chance to say all the unsaid things between us.

Now, Layne Humphrey is one powerful woman; you don't give your word to her lightly about anything. She will hold you accountable until death do you part. I had no phone number for Joey or way to contact him; only sheer intention that he show up to the party. I asked Layne to hold my intention because I knew come hell or high water, she wouldn't let me give up or settle for anything less than Joey showing up and he and I being whole, complete and satisfied in our relationship.

About a week before the party I had a dream. In it I was standing at the front bar in Girard's by the entrance and Joey came around the corner in his big fur coat smiling, like the one he had on his face the last time I saw him.

I bought a dress, rented a limousine, and wrote out invitations to each band member and their significant others. I attached each hand written invitation to a long stemmed pink rose with pink ribbon. I bought half a gram of cocaine and a joint to give to Terry to replace what she had given me when I left The Cenacle behind. Joey's belongings were tucked neatly in a gift bag and off we went to the Baltimore concert.

Jerry, his brother Marc and I rode in the limousine sipping pre-celebratory champagne in anticipation of a wonderful evening. I would deliver the invitations backstage before taking our seats in the concert hall. I had to get the limo into the Civic Center parking garage and myself backstage. When we pulled up to the garage entrance I

159

remembered the sequence of beeps that the limo horns made to have the garage doors open at the venues. The driver sounded the horn as I instructed and the huge steel door opened. Jerry and Marc stayed in the limo while I talked to a security guard and told him why I was there. Gil, wonderful Gil, equipment transportation director for the band (drove the huge semi-truck!) saw me talking to the security guard. He came over, gave me a huge hug and told the guard I was with the band. That old man had a heart of gold.

After catching up, he took me backstage to the VIP guest room where I could leave the invitations and roses. Terry was there and like so many times before, we headed for the ladies room. We caught up; I repaid my debt and gave her Joey's things explaining that if he didn't come to the after party, I wanted to make sure that these things were safely returned to their rightful owner. Terry promised she'd give them to him. She and I were complete.

Jerry, Marc and I left before the encore to get to Girard's to be with our guests and make sure everything was going well. I stood at the front bar waiting for Joey to round the corner as he had in my dream. Layne stood beside me, holding my hand at times with her fully activated faith. Then, Joey entered and rounded the corner in his big fur coat wearing the Joey smile and had his eyes right on me. He stopped in the doorway, I ran to him and we hugged for what seemed like hours but was really just a few minutes. In that hug, everything was forgiven, said and complete with three little words, I love you.

Joey invited us back to his hotel room and we had another intimate after party. We talked, kibitzed, laughed and watched a huge fire from the window in Joey's hotel. A historic Baltimore landmark, The Hecht Company Department Store, caught fire that night and burned to the ground. The painful past was gone and only the ashes of sweet and bitter memories remained.

Later that same year, October 1983, Jerry wanted to vacation in Greece and run the Athens International Marathon while we were there. I'd been running for a while with him and the Werner Erhard inspired organization to bring hunger awareness to the world and end death by starvation, World Runners. I decided I wanted to run the marathon too, but make the miles count and raise money for a second terribly worthy cause, epilepsy.

My doctor refused to sign the medical release form for the marathon, telling me it could cause a breakthrough (re-occurrence) with seizures and I'd be in a foreign country. What the hell would I do then?

I bought a universal epilepsy medical alert bracelet to wear and had another doctor, Mort Orman, also a World Runner, sign the damn paperwork.

It was the original run, starting in the small seaside town of Marathon and extending the hilly 26.2 miles leading to Athens. There'd been a political demonstration that morning so the marathon was three hours late starting, having us run through noontime sun on our way to Athens. More than half of the 1,500 runners dropped out of the race. Determined to make it and meet my financial goal of raising $3,000 for an educational brochure debunking the myths about epilepsy, I kept going. I wasn't about to let all those people who pledged money per mile down and I knew how badly the light needed to be shed on the stigma of epilepsy.

At the 25 mile marker I suffered two shin splints, shouted out in excruciating agony and kept moving toward the finish line. My husband Jerry had finished two hours before me and was running beside me now, cheering me on. My other best friend, Debbie Solesky, was beside him, both telling me I could do it. I started to cry out in pain and kept going. God bless it, I would not be stopped, too much was at stake. This wasn't just about me running my first marathon; this was about showing the world what people can do in spite of their disabilities.

I crossed the finish line with a time of five hours and twenty-seven minutes and collapsed into Jerry's arms. Deep emotion was pouring out of me. I'd done it. By God, I'd done it. Jerry got me to the bleachers, put a blanket over me and held my limp body in his arms. Debbie, kneeling at my broken inhuman looking feet took my shoes off. A kind woman sitting beside me handed me a bottle of water and two aspirin.

Jerry carried me most of the way back to our hotel and put me in bed. It was done; I'd made a difference and when we got back to the US, a fact-based myth busting brochure would be printed and distributed in Maryland public schools.

For as deeply as Jerry and I loved each other, we did not have the essential sexual chemistry necessary for a satisfying marriage. We separated at the end of 1983.

On July 2, 1984, Joey called me at the salon and invited me to come to the show in Columbia, Maryland. I took my mom and we both really enjoyed the show. Joey asked if we would come back the following morning to have brunch with him before he left. I took pictures of the marathon in Greece, newspaper clippings about what I'd achieved, and one of the educational brochures that had been distributed in the public schools as a result of my efforts, so I could share them with Joey.

He said he ran a marathon every night when he performed. While true, I felt slighted; I was hoping he would see what I was achieving in life. When I told him that Jerry and I were divorcing, he said he knew that would happen. I'd married a boy.

Joey and Mom, both with a few years of sobriety now under their belts, talked the walk about AA and the gifts that being sober had brought them. As I listened to them talk I saw the blatant similarities between them. I realized for the first time that many of my romantic choices had been choosing men that had the same flauntingly familiar characteristics as those in the alcoholic and narcissistic home I grew up in.

Joey gave me the Mona Lisa smile just before we left the restaurant and told me that I should grow my hair long, it was too short.

January 7, 1985 Joey called again. This time the concert was at the Baltimore Civic Center and I took Debbie Solesky and Susie Q to the show. We had a marvelous time hanging with the guys.

Mid summer, 1985 Joey called again, while I was entertaining a new love with dinner and champagne. I thanked him for the invitation to come to the show but told him I couldn't possibly make it on such short notice. He called the next day and asked if I would be willing to come see him sometime in Boston. Joey was married and with children now, but not happy in his marriage. He genuinely wanted to spend time with me and I told him that I was willing to visit him if he was willing to tell his wife, April that we would be seeing each other.

He didn't call again until March 7, 1986 when I was six months pregnant.

I went to the show with Susan, and Joey made special arrangements for me to sit beside the sound engineer in the middle of the concert hall so that the baby I was carrying and I would be safe and unharmed from the crowd and the noise. The baby in my belly had been moving a lot before the show but when Aerosmith hit the stage grinding out insanely loud lyrical riffs and pounding bass and drums, my smart little rocker curled up and went to sleep.

Here's how the greatest love of my life came to be.

It was a busy Thursday afternoon in the salon and I was booked with my regular request clients for eyebrow waxings every fifteen minutes. Many of my favorite clients were scheduled back to back.

On this particular late August day in 1985, several of my favorite clients brought their young children with them to the appointment. I remember watching the moms as they interacted with their children. These women, whom I'd only known as professional working women up until now, showed a much softer side as they looked with pride into the eyes of their young, gently correcting them as needed and encouraging them to remain seated nearby.

As I glanced at the faces of their children and into their moms' eyes as they had done, I was overcome with sweet emotion. Their little faces lit up when I smiled at them and I could tell that they trusted me to do whatever it was that I was doing to their moms. I felt privileged to have the children's trust and share a few joyful, loving moments with them and the women, who were the center of their small world.

What a special relationship they had.

I don't know why or how I'd missed this powerful loving bond between parents and children before but I had. I'd been busy working on my career and moving "up" in life as I'd seen my twice divorced parents play the game. I thought that if you worked hard enough, for long enough and collected all the right stuff, then you could consider love, marriage and children.

I was about to turn thirty and I had a list of life goals; buying a house, starting a business, coaching others, having a child, marrying again. Every time I sat down to logically prioritize the list, having a child was always at the top. I know it doesn't make sense and it's not the usual order of events in life, but it's what my heart wanted.

I felt God, a Divine Spirit within me, was in agreement. I know that's a bold-ass statement; thinking we know the Spirit of God and what He wants for our lives, but just the same, I felt it in my soul – at the core of my being.

For five years prior to this, I'd been working with the healing principles, spiritual practices and metaphysical teachings of Louise Hay. I was a student of "A Course in Miracles," "Science of Mind," and had completed most of Werner Erhard's Transformational Courses. I brought most of what I learned into my practice as an esthetician and make-up artist. It naturally spilled over into my personal relationships. I wanted then what I wanted as a child: a world that works for everyone.

Seeing my favorite clients that afternoon with their children, confirmed it for me; having a child was first on my list and an experience that I didn't want to miss.

That night, in my journal, I wrote in red ink,

"I, Nancy Marie Bridge, now warmly and openly receive my man, my mate."

I went to work the next morning forgetting what I'd written in my journal. About midday, as I was busy shaping brows in the front of the salon, a dark haired, skinny, musician-like looking man entered the front door. I felt a whoosh of air from the door opening and heard a playful pounding of big feet coming my way. He was wearing an oversized black raincoat, black pants, a white shirt and a skinny black tie.

He looked rather vampireish with his unusually light for summer skin and long dark hair. Heads were turning to see where this apparition of a man was headed. He smiled as he passed by me and I had an uneasy feeling as I remembered the red inked affirmation I'd written in my journal the night before. No Lord, you can't mean him. Please don't tell me this is who you've sent to bring me a child.

The smell of his cologne lingered in my nose long after he passed by me. I saw an interesting long strapped black bag hanging from his shoulder as he made his way to the back of the salon. He was wearing John Lennon like wire framed glasses and even resembled Lennon with his unusually long nose.

Who was this guy and why was he here?

Next thing I knew he was introducing himself to everyone working in the salon and telling us he'd see us next week, he would be joining us as a hairdresser.

Na, God wouldn't send me a hairdresser to father my child.

Tuesday morning he started work and made a point of playing with everyone's hair, offering to "pump it up a bit." I was busy with clients and not interested in sitting in Romeo's chair.

Mr. Moonlight charmed everyone and I was no exception. Before he left work that first day he invited me to join him and a few of the girls from work for a drink at the nearby Hilton Hotel. I declined, telling him I had a late facial appointment coming in.

Toward the end of giving the facial, my body told me it was hungry for love – or lovemaking. I'd think about it and maybe call someone to come over when I got home. When I finished the facial and quietly opened the door to leave the room, there he was, holding a White Russian in his hand.

"Have a sip, you're done now. Come join us at the Hilton."

Sweet mother of God, protect me from this man.

Divine destiny ruled and I took him home with me. It was the first time in my life that I'd experienced a total, non-vaginal orgasm. He asked if he could call me sometime and I said, "Yes, call around the fourteenth day of my cycle because I know I'm supposed to get pregnant."

165

"Do we have to wait until the 14ᵗʰ? Can't we start earlier? What day is it now?'

I told him that I was serious about having a child and he told me that he was sterile. I duly warned him that being around me, either that little inconvenience would clear up or he'd go away to make room for the person meant to father my child.

Two months later, on a boat under the full Harvest Moon, I got pregnant.

I knew it when it happened. It was if a bright light had entered my satisfied and saturated womb. Lying underneath him, I opened my eyes and said,

"That's it. That was a direct hit. It's a boy and I'll bet you he's born on your birthday."

Where did that come from? Heaven above is all I can say.

On March 14, 1986 Whitney Houston's version of the song, "The Greatest Love," was released as a single record. I was six months pregnant with Dan and couldn't get enough of those lyrics; the greatest love of my life was growing right inside of me. I bought the vinyl album and recorded it on a tape cassette to play in the hospital birthing room.

Four days past my due date, June 27, I went into labor at 11:00 p.m. on a Sunday night. No problem; I got this. I knew for sure that I would simply squat like a Native American Indian and give birth to my precious little papoose in four hours, max. Not a chance, he took his good sweet time. Thirty-six hours later I gave in to the pain of non-stop contractions every four to five minutes, during the non-progressive labor, and took an Epidural and a nap. The fetal monitor woke me up with the needle rocking the redline off the scale, that baby was coming.

I rang for the nurse; she spread my legs for a peek and said it's time to push. Push what? I asked. Having been on an Epidural picnic for four hours, I'd forgotten I was in hard labor. The nurse and both my labor coaches (Layne and her husband, Michael Humphrey), wheeled me to the doorway of the delivery room. The nurse said that only one of them could come in with me. Michael told Layne to go,

I think partly because before I'd had the Epidural I'd almost taken a chunk out of his forearm when I bit it just as he told me to relax and breathe through the pain.

Dan's head was so big. Thank God I abandoned the natural labor plan and surrendered to good drugs.

Beautiful baby boy was born at 2:16 pm on Tuesday afternoon, July 1st, his dad's birthday. He was the most beautiful human I'd ever seen. The music I'd recorded wasn't playing and he didn't cry at first, not until they suctioned his mouth, and then he wailed. I softly uttered my first motherly words to my newborn son,

"Boo, little Boo, I'm right here." He turned his head toward me and stopped crying. It was miraculous how he knew my voice. My voice, the sound of his mother's voice, the one I hoped he'd hear from here to eternity.

Before they cut the umbilical cord I noticed how unusually short it was. I prophetically thought, okay God, I got it; keep this little one on a short leash.

It was so unbelievably hard at first, being unmarried, tired and worn out from the ridiculously long labor and not having a clue what the future would hold for us. I'd read seventeen books about babies, parenting and childrearing while I was pregnant with Dan and nothing prepared me for life that lay ahead of us and the choices I'd have to make being a single parent.

One thing was for certain; my son would be baptized in the church. After numerous futile calls to Christian churches that flat-out turned me down because I wasn't married, I called the Catholic Church where I used to go to dances as teenager. They had two questions: are you Catholic? No, but I had been christened Catholic as a baby and two, is the father Catholic? Yes.

No problem, the sins of the parents have nothing to do with the child. Of course we'll baptize him. I was amazed; the staunch, strict Catholic Church was more than willing to accept this child under God.

Dan's dad did my hair, in my apartment, for the Baptismal ceremony. It was the first time he saw his child and a good excuse for getting him to come over and see him. Shame on me for paying him to do my hair, but I had to see the two of them together, at least once. Daniel had been born on his father's birthday, as I had said he would be, and I wanted his dad to man up or at least acknowledge his existence. He'd been denying that he was the father of my child to everyone that we worked with and our clients for nine months.

As I was changing Dan's diaper his dad couldn't help but notice how well endowed his naked son was. Even as a one month old infant, my son had a huge set of balls. Uneasy, squirming in his own skin the unwilling to be a father man said, "Look, I'm not denying that he's my son – I'm just not ready to take responsibility for that," still looking at Daniel lying naked on the bed.

My new mother's heart was hoping against all odds that he would come around to see the gift of this amazing child lying on my bed and want to be a part of his life.

Meekly, he continued as I was holding my breath and my words at bay.

"Make me one promise. Promise me you will never let him suck his thumb. I don't want his teeth to get all crooked."

Showing him my full and ready to be nursed breasts I told him not to worry, that Daniel had me and takes a ninny.

Placating my nipples he added, "He'll be alright, he's got you. Keep healing the planet. He's living proof of your superpowers."

I invited him to come to the baptism and he decidedly declined.

I grabbed the diaper bag and my gorgeous gift of a son and off we ran to the church, late. Dan was starving and there was no time to nurse him, the guests were seated and the priest, with two attending nuns, was ready to begin.

Daniel began to cry, hard. It didn't help matters that I was holding him so close to my swollen breasts, this child wanted to nurse. No ninny, no finger would satisfy this now howling baby and I wasn't about to whip one out of my blouse in the Catholic Church after they'd been gracious enough to let us in.

Mother's milk stained my shirt as I quietly thanked God and promised to raise my son to know Christ. And Buddha, and art, and music, and every Christ-centered thing I could think of.

I went back to work two weeks later, six weeks after Dan was born. The new business partner (never-been-in-the-business-before boyfriend) of the salon owner, had a meeting with me my first day back on the job. He told me that the conditions for employment with the salon had changed during the short time I was out. There would be no more medical coverage or employer contribution to medical coverage, and if I wasn't able to work a full forty hour week I should seek other employment.

By this time, I had been with the company for almost ten years and had been managing and training the skincare apprentices for two years. I ran the skincare department like I owned it and instilled the best of what I had to offer in my girls. I worked up until the week before I had Dan and I'd spent months introducing my new and proudly trained estheticians to my insanely large clientele. I wanted to make sure the clients were taken care of and knew the girls had my stamp of approval.

Now this well educated moron was pushing me to the brink. I was a new, single and nursing mom and there were no good alternatives for pumping breast milk. Bill Clinton was still the Governor of Arkansas so the Family and Medical Leave Act of 1993 was a far cry away from my existing situation.

I couldn't swing forty hours, pay for child care and run home each day at lunch to feed my newborn. I told him to stick it, went home to my baby and trusted that God would give me a break and show me how to keep a roof over our heads. The salon owner put my cosmetology board license in an envelope and mailed it back to me without a word, a note or return address.

A few months later their entire staff walked out and found jobs at a newly opened salon across the street. Karma is a bitch.

Jerry Bridge, who'd shown up at my door on Rosh Hashanah offering to marry me again and raise Daniel as his own when he found out I was pregnant, gave me a job soliciting leads for him at

169

the Better Business Bureau, allowing me to work from home. Later I did salon consulting which only took me away from Dan for 12-15 hours a week. It all worked out and I got to spend the first two years of my son's life being his fulltime mommy. No better job on the planet.

When Dan was two, I went to work for AVEDA as an educator and account executive proudly wearing the granola, let's save the planet and recycle banner, long before it was the popular or profitable thing to do.

Just before Dan started school, the tiresome 700 miles a week and often out of town traveling was taking its toll on me. I missed Dan so much and didn't want to be so many miles away from him if anything happened and he needed me. I gave notice and accepted a salon esthetician position just before Christmas, 1990.

It lasted one day; I could not work in that particular salon.

I called my friend, Debbie Solesky, who had now opened her own salon and asked her for a job. She said she couldn't bring me in because it would cause conflict amongst her girls, they'd be jealous. We had a Charlie Brown lean Christmas tree that year and just before New Year's Eve I got the bright idea to open my own salon, an AVEDA salon. Dan had two twelve inch magic play wands with glittery swirling particles inside them. I took one, asked my mom to baby-sit and drove downtown determined that I would find a space to rent and open a business. I now had a magic wand!

I parked on Charles Street and walked inside of historic Brown's Arcade. There was a woman in the back storefront picking up paper trash inside the small empty space. I asked her if she knew whether or not the space was for rent. She told me it was as she'd just moved her shop up to the front of the arcade. Writing the leasing agent's name down for me, she said I should call him soon because the space probably wouldn't last long. It hadn't been listed yet.

I reached the leasing agent as he was leaving for the airport and quickly told him of my idea. He told me where to send a letter of interest. Done. I was going for it, and that space would be mine.

By the Grace of God and financial help from my mother, I wrote and typed a 78-page business plan, secured a small business loan from a bank and negotiated a 68-page lease with the huge conglomerate, The Rouse Company who built Baltimore's Inner Harbor.

Tucara Salon opened for business on April 13, 1991.

Tucara Salon was like the triumphant train in the children's book, "The Little Train That Could." In a very small 756 square feet we generated a quarter of a million dollars in revenue with a fifty percent sales to service ratio, meaning that fifty percent of the money came from retail sales, within the first two years.

In the third year that Tucara was open, 1994, we began to attract a celebrity film clientele. I have no idea how that happened other than what one guest told me; Tucara Salon had been placed on a Film Screen Recommendation List as a preferred salon to visit in Baltimore for salon services. Who was I to argue?

Actually, now that I think about it, it may have been Margaret Hilliard, a film production manager, who came in for services earlier that same year. Margaret worked on the movie, "Serial Mom" filmed in Baltimore.

Small business computers and software were beginning to hit the market but I preferred to manage Tucara with the use of a cash register and a paper appointment book for scheduling clients. I've always enjoyed the smell of freshly sharpened pencils and any reason to visit an office supply or stationary store.

My mom had scheduled an appointment for "Elizabeth Taylor" to have a facial with me. It wasn't really Elizabeth Taylor. Mom said she couldn't quite catch the name but it was someone from a movie that was being filmed in Baltimore.

Tucara had an all-glass exterior wall on the front so you could see guests for twenty or so feet before they actually entered the front door. I was sitting on a tall chair behind the reception desk waiting for Elizabeth to arrive when I noticed a lanky young girl bustling toward the door. She had a definite rhythmic strut to her long gated walk. I know that walk, I thought; I've seen this walk before.

The wheels of my mind began to toggle backwards as I watched her make her way to the salon entrance.

Her head bobbed up and down each time her long legs moved forward. She was smiling at me as she approached the door. I know this walk, I know this walk, who the hell is she? As she pulled the front door open it hit me. She walks like Steven Tyler.

"Hi, I'm here for a facial, with Nancy, I think."

"Yes, hello, I'm Nancy. I'm afraid we've gotten your name wrong. You're not Elizabeth Taylor."

"No, I'm not! My name is Liv Tyler."

Holy shit… it's Steven's daughter.

I shook her hand, welcomed her to Tucara and asked if she needed to use the ladies room before we began her treatment.

Once inside the facial room, I could see just how much she resembled both Steven and Bebe – but all that sweetness – where did that come from?

An AVEDA candle was burning in the room, making delicious smelling shadows on the wall. An angel sculpture sat high on a corner shelf peering down at us. I gave her instructions as to how to put on the facial gown, where to put her belongings and how to get up and onto the facial bed. I stepped out of the room so she could get ready.

I prayed, "Dear Lord in Heaven, help me to know how to best serve this beautiful young creature and when to tell her about the plane, knowing her parents and the difference that flight made in my life."

A few minutes later, I stepped back into the facial room and cocooned her in a warm blanket making sure to tuck it under her feet with a gentle squeeze. I lifted her head, comfortably resting on a white towel, pulled her long brown hair upward and out of the way as I lovingly swaddled her head in the towel. I placed a few drops of AVEDA lavender essential oil under her nose and asked her to take a few deep breaths. Next I spread a pre-warmed cleansing cream over her face and neck. She looked up at me and said,

"You have the most wonderful touch…"

You've got to be kidding me. This beautiful, Walt Disney woodland princess, all of sixteen years old, is looking up at me complimenting my touch? Breathe Nan, keep breathing and infuse love into this precious child. You have a gift for her.

Liv was the lovechild of Steven and Bebe whose energy I first felt on that small chartered plane in the Midwest when Joey was being such a turd. Like most of us, I didn't know of her existence until she was about ten years old. Bebe ended her affair with Steven, went back to Todd Rundgren and they raised Liv as their own biological child.

I'd read in a People magazine that Liv figured it out after seeing Steven a few times. She was undeniably a well-loved child.

She almost fell asleep with the facial mask on while I was giving her an arm and hand massage. I left the facial mask on an extra ten minutes after placing her hands in heated mittens. I tip-toed out of the room and wondered how I'd tell her about knowing her parents. She was so beautiful; I prayed that the right words would find me.

I returned to the room with a glass of spring water for her and carefully removed the facial mask; rousing her ever so slightly back to reality, as I removed the towel from around her head I asked her how she was doing.

"Won-der-ful," she said.

"Good, I'm glad."

I sat her up and rubbed her back for a few minutes before walking around to the side of the bed where I could see her face, right side up, and give her the water.

"That was the best facial I've ever had," she complimented.

"I'm so glad that you enjoyed it."

She told me about working on the movie, "Silent Fall." It was her first film and she was really happy to be acting. She talked about her experience of working with greats like Richard Dreyfuss and Linda Hamilton and how very fortunate she considered herself to be.

"Liv," I began, "I know your parents. I was onboard a small plane with them out in the Midwest when they were first pregnant with you. I was Joey Kramer's girlfriend, the drummer in Aerosmith. I was a Playboy Bunny in Boston and often traveled with the band."

Eyes still sleepy, yawning and trying to comprehend what I was telling her, she looked at me puzzled.

I started again, "Your mom and dad were dating way back when and we were on a small chartered plane in the Midwest, and Aerosmith, the band, was on tour. Your mom and I were traveling with them."

She looked totally confused and bewildered.

"This was when your mom wasn't with Todd. She and your dad, Steven, whom I knew quite well because of the band, Aerosmith, were dating. Joey, the drummer of the band, was my boyfriend."

Her eyes widened and she nodded her head in agreement.

I continued, "Your mom and dad were on this plane with us, nestled together in the back of the plane. They were both wearing huge fur coats, laughing, cuddling, very much in love. Joey and I were in the front. Your parents were so happy and deeply in love. You, my dear, were in your mom's belly. I've never seen two people more in love."

She began to cry.

Grabbing a tissue for her I asked her why she was crying.

"They've always told me that they were happy when I was conceived, but I've never actually talked to anyone or met anyone other than the two of them, who was actually there."

"Sweet girl, I've never seen two happier people. I've never forgotten the impression their love made on me and I never will."

I told her about the precious little fur balls covered in love and blissfully lost in a world of their own and how I wanted to be in that world with them. I told her about the difference it made in my life to witness the two of them together. She laughed when I told her what a stinker Joey had been on that flight.

More happy tears fell and she gushed with joy hearing the story.

It was almost dark when she left the salon so I walked her outside and watched her as she made her way down the hill and toward her hotel.

Liv visited Tucara a few more times, enjoying other services and on her last visit she asked me at the door as she was leaving, "Why do you watch me walk back to my hotel? I'm safe; I've lived in cities before."

"Because you are a friend's daughter and I know they would do the same for me."

She hugged me and said, "People from your generation, yours and my Dad's, are so kind. Thank you, thank you, for everything."

I watched her walk down the hill one last time and gave thanks for the blessings covering her life. She'd also been born on July 1st.

In the summer of 1997, I went to see Richard to have my hair done. He'd returned from LA and was banging it out with hair in Bethesda, Maryland. Even though I owned a salon and could have any of the stylists do my hair, I wanted to get out of Baltimore, see Richard, and be treated like a client. Richard always seemed to re-enter my life at important times and with doubling the square footage of Tucara, I felt this was one of those times; I needed a dose of Richard.

It was a busy bustling Saturday at "David's Beautiful People Salon" and I was so excited to just be a client in the salon; not an owner or worker. Richard suggested coloring my hair, which I rarely did and trusting his mastery, I let him. He gave me a few magazines to read while the color processed. Each current issue of the fashion magazines had a picture of Julia Roberts on the front cover with stunning headlines that the actress was about to turn thirty in October. All of the front cover headshots of Julia were unflattering, as far as I was concerned, because the beautiful Julia Roberts had eyebrows that, in my opinion, had been hacked and whacked. I was tremendously upset that, for all the beauty she possessed, no one was noticing or paying attention to the lady's eyebrows. How could you miss it? I couldn't get past seeing such a pretty woman with horribly misshaped eyebrows.

Richard came over to check the hair color that was processing on my head and I pointed out the travesty of Julia's brows. I guess in trying to calm me down, Richard suggested we add some of the same hair color on my head to my eyebrows. Five minutes later he returned and I was still furrowing my brow about how such a travesty could happen when the woman had more eyebrow hair to start with than a

Middle Eastern man. Richard said if I felt that strongly about it, why didn't I do something? Of course he would say that; that was Richard, don't complain, tell me what you're gonna do to fix it.

Without hesitation, I boldly declared out loud to Richard, "I will do Julia Robert's eyebrows and give her the most beautiful brows she's ever had."

Richard said, "Good, problem solved. You're done, color's ready to come off, let's get you shampooed."

I left the salon feeling wonderful, beautiful and empowered.

A year later, in August of 1998, I completed the Landmark Forum Advanced Course which evolved from the EST 6-Day Course. I'd been reunited with the powerful context of living life as my word and calling things into being from nothing other than one's word; a very powerful place to stand in life. I'd totally forgotten about the declaration I'd made to Richard about doing Julia's eyebrows. I was doing my best to manage a business, a team of talented professionals, and being a single mom to a budding boy. In many ways I felt that my twelve year-old son was being short-changed with time with his mom and being his mom was the most important job I had.

I set an after school date with him where I would pick him up from school rather than him taking the bus home and we would just hang out and be together before dinner. On that September day, film producer Margaret Hilliard called me in the salon. We'd met a few years earlier when she was in Baltimore with "Serial Mom." Margaret said that she was in town with a movie and needed me to do someone's brows. I told her about the date with my son and that I absolutely could not disappoint him. I assured her that one of my staff would do an excellent job for her. She persisted that no, she needed me for this assignment. Having full faith in my staff, trained by me, I apologized again and told Margaret I simply wasn't available.

Margaret, half whispering into the phone said, "Nancy, you must do it. It's Julia Roberts."

With that, I agreed to go pick up my son from school and bring him back to the salon with me. While driving to Dan's school

I remembered what I'd said to Richard about doing Julia's brows. Dang, this shit really works!

My son and I both had loved Julia Roberts since we first saw her in the hopeful romantic comedy, "Pretty Woman." I'd bought the VHS tape and we'd watched it numerous times with the same fantasy, maybe one day my knight in shining armor might gallantly ride up on a studly white horse to marry us. I decided not to tell Daniel who the important client was that required me to return to the salon.

When we got back to the salon I pointed to a chair and told Daniel to take a seat and get started on his homework. What a good lad he was; he had no idea that the actress he had a crush on was about to walk in for an appointment with his mom. He sat down and opened his books. I brought him a snack and as Julia was walking through the door he almost choked on his water. I smiled, excused myself and told him I'd be back shortly.

Julia brought her make-up artist, Richard Dean, with her to the appointment. I felt right at home with her but I wasn't used to a Hollywood make-up artist looking over my shoulder as I shaped brows. The pressure was on. They chatted about the movie they were making, "Runaway Bride," the different scenes, how her make-up should look and all the bridal gowns she'd be wearing. Julia, remembering that there would be a close-up shot of a kiss with Richard Gere that week, asked if I would wax her upper lip too.

Not wanting to hurt her delicate skin, I used a more gentle wax that didn't remove all of the soft, light hairs on her upper lip. I asked her make-up artist who was now quite relaxed and no longer looking over my shoulder, to take a peek and see if it was okay. He agreed the peach fuzz that was left wouldn't show up on the film and her brows were fantastic.

Leaving the facial room we came around the corner into the retail area and Daniel was standing with his back to us, pretending to be looking at the AVEDA products on the shelf. We stopped and I introduced my awestruck awesome son to Julia Roberts. What an incredible moment. I'm not sure which I enjoyed more, shaping her eyebrows or the look on Daniel's face when he met her.

The next time I saw Julia was just after filming the introduction scene where she's riding on horseback in a bridal gown. She said they'd had her riding the horse for twelve hours and that every muscle in her body ached. I gave her a two hour massage and a receipt for service to be submitted to Workman's Compensation. Not only was she beautiful, she was smart and wasn't about to let anyone take advantage of her.

I had the pleasure of being her esthetician for five months while she was in Baltimore filming the movie. I found her to be delightfully sweet, genuine and down to earth; often times bringing a knitting project with her to the salon. I admired the closeness she had with her family and the intelligence she executed in keeping them nearby for love and support.

I also found Julia to be a non-linear thinker like myself. She didn't merely surmise that one plus one plus one equals three as in a logical thinking perspective, she thought in terms of what else is possible. Life doesn't just occur in a sequentially straight line; there are turns, twists and circles to be discovered. I enjoyed our conversations immensely and I'd like to think that she remembers a few of them or at least me, fondly.

I share this story with you not to brag, rather to point to the power of making bold-ass declarations fueled by passion and desire accompanied with belief in yourself for what's possible. When you live life from being your word in the universe rather than the character in your story, you are able to see yourself as something bigger than your ego or personality. When you hold yourself accountable for your life and everything that occurs in it, the magic wand is in your hands. You have the power to create. Or destroy. Or invent a life you love.

Never believe you're the character in your story. You're the one telling it. How do you say it's turned out? It really is up to you and, by the way, it's already turned out exactly the way it was meant to unfold. This is where faith in something bigger than you comes into play. My six year old son once asked me how big God was. We were riding in the car and he was gazing out the window looking up at the sky, seemingly trying to gain a relative understanding of the size of God.

My answer, "Bigger than the sky you're looking at, son."

Thinking God may have a human form, Dan replied, "Jeez – He must have the biggest butt in the whole world!"

I assured him it was so.

Each of us determines who God is for ourselves or what is the entity that is larger than the flesh sack that houses our bodies and minds. For me, it is the trinity of God, Jesus and the Holy Spirit. And I believe that the Creator gave us minds and free will so that we could figure this stuff out and ultimately choose to believe in Him. I won't apologize for my faith; neither will I try to convert you to my way of thinking. I would encourage you to consider who God is for you as only you can answer that question for yourself.

For me, I'm humbled before a God that has the biggest butt in the whole world. He is the ruler, creator and inventor of all things. Nothing happens to us unless it goes before Him first. I believe He knows every hair on our head before we're even born and all the trials and tribulations we'll go through. I also think He knows all the mistakes we'll make and loves us just the same.

God, for me, intimately knows our strengths, weaknesses and defects of character and loves us all equally – in spite of ourselves. This is the power I choose to tap into with all the knowledge, wisdom and sometimes understanding, that He'll grant along the way.

My biggest challenge has been learning to love myself the way He loves me; wholly and unconditionally. For the longest time, I judged myself and determined my self worth based on the experiences and events in my life. When I thought of things like running a marathon, giving famous people personal services or dating a rock star, my self-esteem rose. When I recounted mistakes I'd made, places where I'd failed or the fact that I'd been molested and raped, my self-esteem went to hell.

Good, bad or indifferent – all of these thoughts are interpretations of the actual occurrences in my life and have nothing to do with personal value. Who I am is who I say I am and I choose to align with

179

what God says about me. I am a beautiful and precious human being who is known, loved and cherished by Him. I'm neither the character nor the victim in the story of my life. I'm the story-teller.

One afternoon, just before Dan's tenth birthday, we were sitting on the couch in our living room following a school field trip. I'd taken the day off and gone along to help chaperone the fourth graders at an industrial quarry. An overweight, loud and obnoxious pre-menstrual girl from his class had teased the hell out of him about not having a dad, with me sitting on the bus next to him. It took everything I had not to whack her and give her a well-deserved tongue lashing. Dan's teacher told me it wasn't the first time Dan had been teased about not knowing his dad. She said that even though other students came from homes with divorced parents, the difference was that they saw them. Usually Monday mornings were filled with kids chatting about what they'd done over the weekend with the non-custodial parent.

It broke my heart. I'd always lived in places with the best public schools so that Dan would get a good education and this was the second time he was being singled out for not having a dad in the home. When it happened in third grade, I moved to an even better neighborhood because they had a more accurate demographic of divorced families.

Dan was sad, sitting next to me on the couch, crying.

"Why don't I have a dad? Why doesn't he come to see me? Play with me, send me a card for my birthday?"

I told him that sometimes God doesn't give you certain things so that you can learn from other things. Satisfied with my answer, Dan boldly declared,

"When I grow up, I'm going to be the best dad in the world. I'm going to play with my kids and take them places. I'm gonna have four kids, two girls and two boys."

Really creating it now, he continued.

"And I'm gonna go to college in Colorado and be a snowboard instructor and a chef."

My mind raced to tally the total for out-of-state college tuition and how the hell would I ever be able to afford that big-ass dream? I kept quiet.

I let him sit there and dream, dream as big as he wanted to. Who was I to squelch his dreams? I'd given him Dr. Ben Carson's book, "Think Big" when he was in the first grade, followed by Helen Keller's story. No, I wouldn't be dream killing anything this beautiful boy cared to create for himself. I kept my small minded mouth shut and let him fly.

I remembered the argument he'd gotten into with the pre-school teacher when he was three. The kids were instructed to cut out magazine pictures of who lived in their home and paste them onto a construction paper house. Dan chose a little boy wearing a cowboy hat to represent himself and an attractive, young sexy woman to represent me, and his dad. The teacher told him that the woman couldn't be both; she had to be his mom and only his mom; he was wrong.

Dan went balls to the wall arguing with the teacher and defending the fact that his mommy was both! Yes, this beautiful woman in the picture was both, his mommy and his daddy. That's how he saw the world at that time. And there wasn't a damn thing wrong with his point of view.

A couple of years later, sitting around a kitchen table at Cub Scouts, the little Tiger Cub boys were asked how many brothers and sisters they each had. Most of them had younger siblings, mostly sisters. When it was Dan's turn, he confidently informed the group,

"Well, I don't have any little sisters, but me and my Ma, we're gonna adopt."

What a beautiful way to see the world; anything was possible.

After Dan got it all out on the couch we went outside and threw some balls on the side of the house. He was good. He'd tucked his big dream visions for his future safely away, somewhere inside of his heart.

The next day, when he went to school and the overweight little Miss I'm Gonna Make Your Life Miserable started in on him again, he politely suggested that she go out and buy a Nordic Track treadmill and call Jenny Craig at 1-800-GO JENNY. That's my boy, well mannered, matter of fact and use your brain not your brawn.

When Dan was fourteen and just starting high school I closed Tucara Salon. I'd had enough of working seventy hours a week and being a 24/7 mother to children I hadn't given birth to. I was burned out and my teenage son needed a mom who could be fully available to him during those tough teenage years which were about to hit hard and heavy.

During the ten years I'd had Tucara I often dreamed of closing it one day and returning to Miami Beach to do just brows. I found an esthetician's position at an AVEDA salon on South Beach and moved back to my Miami, the fun and sun capital of the world. This was in July of 2001.

I was slowly building a clientele on the Beach, trusting that when September came, so would the tourists. I'd promised my son, an avid snowboarder, that even though we were now living in Miami he could still fly north twice a month during snowboard season for competitions.

One seemingly typical blue skied Miami morning, as I was leaving for work, the gardener of the complex where we were living came running toward the building as I was walking to my car. With his hands on top of his head he shouted in very broken English, "America, America she being attacked. Dios mio."

It was about 9:15 a.m. I couldn't understand what he was trying to tell me.

"New York, bombs. Trade Center bombs, go listen to radio."

I hurried to my car, turned on the radio, but couldn't find a news station.

When I walked into the salon fifteen minutes later the radio was on and was reporting that America was under attack. And, downtown Miami was shut down due to a bomb reportedly being placed in a large bank.

I raced to Miami Beach High to get Dan. Cars and fleeing parents were everywhere, jamming the parking lot. Warning sirens were sounding and people were running in and out of the school.

Inside, the school's administrators were demanding that identification be shown to pick up your child. I'd left my purse in the car and screamed at an official when she refused to send my son to the office unless I provided proof that I was his mother.

I ran back to the car, got my driver's license and pushed my way to the front of the line waving it at the woman who'd tried to stand between me and my son. I told her she'd best get him now. She did.

Not knowing what we were facing or how long this would go on, I drove to the Publix Market and we picked up non-perishable food, bottled water, batteries and candles. Remembering that we had elderly neighbors, Dan put more supplies in the grocery cart so we'd have enough to share.

When we got home, Peter Jennings was at his desk reporting from where he would remain for thirty-six hours. F-1 American fighter jets flew over our building on the bay, hourly, that entire day and into the next.

My salon boss called two days later and said that he was sorry but no one would be traveling to Miami and he couldn't afford to keep me on salary.

Planes were grounded and if and when the air traffic ban lifted, there would be no way that I would allow my son to get on a flight without me. I packed up and moved us back to Baltimore.

At forty-seven years old I went to work as a waitress in a newly opened sports bar where I wouldn't have to confront people who'd known the salon owner and esthetician I had once been.

In 2004, About Faces offered me a position and I accepted it, in their flagship location, as a sales representative who would help to drive their retail sales to a new level.

Daniel, having graduated from high school, registered for classes at the community college and I signed up too. I registered for four classes, including English 101. God bless it, I wanted to pass that English course and get a college degree. Otherwise, how would anyone ever take me seriously as a writer? I'd been seizure free for a number of years and even though I was working full-time in a new job, I thought I could handle it. Two weeks into the semester I was overwhelmed, over my head and I began to have seizures again. I thought it would be different this time because of the 1990, "Individuals with Disabilities Education Act," section 504, which serves to protect and aid students with disabilities. It may have helped, had I not been working forty to fifty hours a week. I failed again.

Dan continued and after three semesters, he came home one afternoon, just before Christmas 2005, and informed me that he'd accepted a job in Colorado as a snowboard instructor at a ski resort and would be moving in January. He also said that after the ski season he planned to stop by the University of Colorado, find the coach for the collegiate snowboard team and talk to him about being on the team. If the coach thought he had a shot of making the team, he'd do whatever it took to become a permanent resident of Colorado, pay tuition and graduate with a four year degree.

My boy, could I possibly be any prouder? He made it happen. He ate a lot of beans and rice and lived in cold damp Colorado basements, but he made it happen. He graduated from the University of Colorado in Boulder, in May of 2011, and I was there to witness the momentous occasion.

Umberto

Richard

White Knight

A Man With a Snake—Kyf Brewer

January 31, 1981
My Third Jewish Drummer and
The Only One I Married

Me and Jerry
on a Mission

Transformed Souls

187

A Blazing View From Joey's Hotel Room

Why Am I Still
Stuck in the
Middle With You?

Great Show With
Steven, Susan, Brad
and Me

Mother Nature's Son

Double Your Pleasure

ET Take Me Home!

Auntie Layne and Daniel

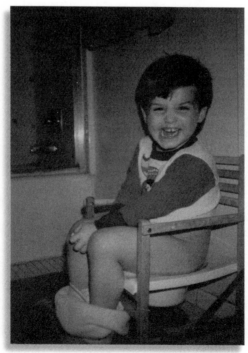

First Poop in a Pot

What's Not to Love About Jewish Drummers?
Jerry Bridge and Michael Kaplan

Layne and the Boys

Track **10**

BIG, BRAVE, BEAUTIFUL HEARTS
– Hitting the Big Time!

I've always wanted to write and tell stories from the time I could hold a big fat Crayon. I would write full length plays (in my mind) and orchestrate all the parts and costumes and act them out for anyone who would give me the time of day.

One Sunday afternoon, at my Norwegian grandpa's house in Miami, I was giving my best performance to my Grandpa and his beer drinking buddy when they burst out into howling laughter. I know now that they weren't laughing at me, but at the time I thought it was me. They were howling within their own inattentive to me conversation and it wasn't a funny scene.

I ran from the house, through the neighborhood and hid under a plywood makeshift structure that sat on cement blocks. I cried my little eyes out and made friends with the bugs and lizards who kept me company. I was missing for hours and no one noticed. I returned home as the sun was setting only to be told that I'd missed supper.

No more plays for me – but I couldn't help telling stories. Everything that I saw, heard and experienced was translated in my beautiful childlike mind with an internal narration.

Well into adulthood, I was aware of the inner workings of my observant mind to tell a story in the best possible way that would be clearly understood by the listener.

I failed high school English in my senior year. I didn't pass the required Review English in college, the first, second or even the third time I tried. I gave up – but I never stopped writing. I've always known I'm a writer, but up until now, the Universe just never outwardly agreed with me.

In 2012, shortly after my dear friend Laura Kaufman died, I walked smack dab into a glass wall at a friend's wedding and suffered a severe head, neck and back injury. Intricate surgery was required to correct the damage. My father passed away the week prior to the surgery. I couldn't work for six months.

I went back to work in October, 2012, for one amazing week, and set a new sales record for individual sales. I cried each morning and every night from debilitating pain in my spine that was not yet totally fused back together. My body could no longer withstand the standing, moving, bending and smiling required to get my job done.

I resigned, cashed in my meager assets and moved to a small island off the Gulf Coast of Texas, where my dad had once lived, determined to finish my book in a year. It felt as if this was where God was calling me to go and finally finish what I'd started.

Texas was a bust after three weeks. Nothing was as I thought it would be. I couldn't find work or an affordable place to live and I couldn't go home. I'd rented my home out for a year to finish the book. I felt like God had abandoned me, leaving me to wander the desert for forty years.

I traveled 7,000 miles in a complete circle around the country in a U-Haul truck towing my car, writing materials and kitty cat behind it, not knowing where I was supposed to land. I sat on a lot of street curbs with the truck parked next to me confused, crying, and journaling my fear. What the hell had I done? Where was I supposed to be and how was I ever going to finish this book?

Heartbroken, deeply depressed, wet, skinny and angry with God, I returned to Baltimore eight weeks later and landed on a dear friend's doorstep. Mona took us in (me and Twinks, my kitty) broken dreams and all, and nursed us both back to health.

For months I couldn't open a journal, a notebook or even my computer. I was grieving the loss of many things, but mostly the dream of writing a book. I had pages and pages and dozens of notebooks filled with stories that I thought would never be told.

Mona continued to feed and encourage me, assuring my lost and wretched soul that I'd recover. She never gave up on me.

It also appeared to my set-the-world-on-fire environmentalist son that I'd failed miserably. I had. I could hardly bear to pick up the phone when he'd call and I'd hear in his voice that he was worried about his mother's future. I was a middle-aged parent and this wasn't supposed to happen. Kids cash in and follow dreams, not old farts like me. How could I have been so stupid, was the consensus from everyone I knew. I hated to see the pity in their eyes when they'd look at me.

I'd taken all my fancy framed certificates, achievement awards and diplomas from Esthetic Schools and the AVEDA Institutes out of their frames and put them in a never to be seen again folder when I moved to Texas. I was never going back to the cosmetic industry again; I was going to be a published writer.

I could now barely look at my face in the mirror but my friend, Mona, looked at it everyday and told me how much she loved me and believed that I'd get back up again.

Mona, older, wiser and no stranger to heartbreak herself promised me that this would pass and reminded me that I was a gift to many people, I'd just forgotten. In time, I would heal and remember.

As I began to share my stories and beaten down dreams with her, she recounted the many things I'd already accomplished in my life. She told me something that I'd never heard or known before; that all one person needs is someone to believe in them. She understood, better than anyone ever had, that sometimes we fail miserably and some wounds never completely heal.

Mona heard me, I mean really heard me, when I told her about Joey and how much I had loved him and how deeply hurt I'd been after reading his book. I shared a few chapters that I'd written for my book with her and she lovingly told me that it was time to share my story; maybe it could help someone else and would definitely help to heal my broken and battered spirit.

It was time for me to embrace my whole heart and all that I've ever wanted to do, to be a force of Nature instead of a selfish little clot of ailments complaining that the world would not devote itself to making me happy.

"I am of the opinion that my life belongs to the whole community and as long as I live it is my privilege to do for it whatever I can. I want to be thoroughly used up when I die, for the harder I work the more I live. I rejoice in life for its own sake. Life is no 'brief candle' for me. It is a sort of splendid torch which I have got hold of for the moment, and want to make it burn as brightly as possible before handing it on to future generations."

Thank you, Mr. George Bernard Shaw and Mr. Joey Kramer.

What I've learned is that a writer is something you become after a lot of hard work and practice, and I've been practicing my ever-loving Bunny tail off to share this tale with you.

In my thirties when I was raising my son as a single parent, I had a vision of myself, as a child. I saw myself (in black and white) as a little girl with both knees knocked out and bandaged. The child in me was smiling and hobbling toward the adult me. I cried to see this wounded and damaged child missing vital parts as she continued to walk in my direction. I wanted to take her into my arms and tell her how lovely she was.

It seemed to me that she didn't know she was lacking two functional knees on her small legs which made me cry even more. She just kept moving toward me on her tiny crutches.

When she reached me I smiled and took her into my arms. Nothing was wrong with her. As far as she was concerned, the world was a happy and beautiful place.

I interpreted her knees to represent her two parents; wounded, missing and unable to support her in life. She kept moving forward just the same and became the best damn set of parents for herself as she possibly could.

A few years after that young vision of myself, I had a realization about 'single parenting.' I'd always professed that I'd raised my son by myself and that it was difficult.

"Well, I'm a single mom, cut me some slack."

"Well, he doesn't have a father in the home. Forgive the lad."

"Life is tough as a single parent and you'd better make an exception for me and my boy. Have pity on us."

Lies. Misconceptions. Caca del toro. I was never alone. God was always there, providing, protecting and guiding us through those tumultuous teenaged years, especially. It took wisdom and understanding after the fact, to see that it was so. We were never alone; it just felt like it most of the time.

Parenting is tough no matter what the circumstances. It's a crap shoot. You do your absolute best to give them a happy childhood and like you and me, they only get one. Make it count. Make it the best damn childhood for them you possibly can.

As babies, toddlers and adolescents they will continue to break your heart wide open to the point where you think you can't possibly hold any more love, cuteness and affection.

At some point in their maturation process they will hurt you deeply. They will break your ever-loving heart into a million pieces and rip it out of your chest. Let them; it's their job. I was lucky with Dan, he told me just after he started to grow hair on his face that he was angry with me. He said he couldn't explain it and didn't know why but had a feeling that things were going to change between us. Boy, did they ever! It's a miracle we both survived his teenage years.

Remember this about children: they won't be yours forever. They'll find their own path, their own life's mission and leave. Yes, they will leave your happy home and God willing, take all the love you've given them and share it with the rest of the world.

As parents, be there, hold their hands in the car and freeze those precious moments in time. God willing, your children will continue to grow and leave you with a treasure chest of precious memories, frozen in time.

Have their backs, always, well into their adulthood. Speak blessings and praise over them, forever. I've heard it said that when parents pray for their children the choir of angels in Heaven stops singing and God bends His ear down toward Earth to hear our prayers. I believe it's true.

I've also learned to love and speak blessings over myself, like I do my son.

We've all got our own lot to carry, cross to bear, life to live, Karma to catch and dreams to chase. I wouldn't trade it for anything.

Life is a marathon and the best we can do is run our own race. Every time we take the stage (get up in the morning) we run a marathon.

The cheering crowds on the side of the road, in the audience or sitting next to you wouldn't be applauding if they didn't recognize their own magnificence in what they see in you. So get over your rockstar self and reach for that place deep inside of you that only champions know about when you've got nothing left to give. Reach into that sanctuary of human awesomeness and pull it out. You're an amazing human being, as great as they come.

You choose, you chart your course no matter what you've been given; everybody's been given something.

As for me, I'm learning to play the drums and continuing to practice writing books. I love my wild-ass born to rock self. This is the legacy I choose to leave my son and the world. Getting old doesn't suck, mean people suck. Old people rock!

I hate to fail but I'm damn good at it. I'm also good at winning.

Dream on…Keep dreaming…

Dream until your dreams come true!

About the Author

Nancy Karlson Bridge is on a mission to help people transform their experience of themselves and fully embrace their own and others' magnificence.

Nancy has been on a transformation path for more than thirty-five years. She has completed more than one hundred transformational workshops, seminars and leadership training programs through Erhard Seminars Training and Landmark Education.

Never having run a distance of more than ten miles in her life, Nancy ran in, and completed, a 26.2 mile international marathon in Athens, Greece. She did this to raise awareness about the abilities of people with epilepsy and to collect contributions for a desperately needed fact-based, myth-busting brochure that was distributed in Maryland public schools. Nancy also served on the Board of Directors for the Epilepsy Association of Maryland.

She has been featured in both print and television media for her achievements as a self-disclosed consumer and advocate, for persons with disabilities as well as her expertise as an esthetician, brow guru and owner of an award winning AVEDA Concept salon in Baltimore.

Nancy Karlson Bridge

Her proudest accomplishment is having given birth to an amazing, set- the-world-on-fire environmentalist son. He is a deeply cherished and most loved child by choice, born to a single mom.

Life is no brief candle to Nancy. It is a sort of 'splendid torch' which she has hold of and intends to make burn as brightly as possible before handing it on to future generations.

Nancy is completing a children's book about children's natural ability to know the presence of the Divine and is also currently working on a third book.

Read more about Nancy and her work on
www.nancykarlsonbridge.com